The Russian Tragedy

The Russian Tragedy
Alexander Berkman

The Russian Tragedy
Alexander Berkman
First published as three separate pamphlets by
Der Syndicalist, Berlin, 1922.
Published as one book by Cienfuegos Press,
Orkney, 1976, 0-904564-11-8.
Published in this edition by Phoenix Press, London,
1986, 0-948984-00-7.

Text printed and book bound
by A Wheaton & Co Ltd., Exeter.

Phoenix Press
BM Bookserv
London WC1N 3XX

Introduction

Russia is a dictatorship. It is a class society with massive restrictions on freedom of speech and even on freedom of movement. Those who object to this state of affairs risk imprisonment or worse. All this is beyond question. What is questionable, however, is the political philosophy where all the injustices condemned in Communist countries are excused provided they are done in non-Communist countries in the name of anti-Communism.

Anyone who can simultaneously excuse injustice in one country and condemn it in another obviously has no genuine objection to injustice and so the explanation for the phenomenon of anti-Communism must be found somewhere other than in revulsion at the nature of Communist countries. In fact anti-Communists use the existence of Communist dictatorships to divert attention from everything that is wrong in their own societies. In particular, they find it convenient to believe that their own dissidents are all Communists. Parroting why-don't-you-go-back-to-Russia? sidesteps confronting the accusations and arguments of the West's dissidents. Or perhaps anti-Communists are honestly incapable of realising that it is possible to reject both East and West.

On the other hand are those who have fooled themselves into believing that Russia is the workers' paradise. This is just as ridiculous a philosophy as anti-Communism and, as with anti-Communism, the reason why people believe in it is to be found outside of the philosophy itself. Anyone repelled by part of Western society will find it comforting to believe that just round the corner is a society where everything they object to in the West has been put right. And if emotion is allowed to prevail over honesty then the reality of Russia can be transformed into an attractive fantasy. So the fraud of anti-

Communism is opposed by the delusion of the workers' paradise. Getting back to reality, the nature of Communist societies is clear and the important question to answer is how Communist societies, beginning with Russia, came into being.

The First World War brought slaughter to the soldiers of the Russian Army and starvation to the Russian people. Early in 1917 they revolted against the Tsar's dictatorship. Soldiers mutinied, peasants took over the land they worked and workers took over their factories. A provisional government tried to prop up the crumbling old order by introducing parliamentary democracy but with the armed forces no longer loyal the situation passed out of the government's control. In October 1917 Kerensky's provisional government was swept away.

There had been a social revolution in Russia but its future was unclear. On top of massive economic problems supporters of the old Tsarist dictatorship had formed armies to destroy the revolution. Those who had fought to overthrow the Tsarist system prepared to resist and among them were the Bolsheviks, a Marxist party whose actions are to be understood by reference to the economic and political ideas that Karl Marx had set out the previous century.

The essence of Marx's failed attempt to establish scientific socialism is as follows; in the advanced capitalist countries the industrial working class, the proletariat, will become poorer and poorer and more and more numerous until they are the overwhelming majority of the population. They will then overthrow the capitalist system through revolution and all means of production will be centralised in the hands of a new government. (This is called the dictatorship of the proletariat, a curious appellation since the proletariat are supposed to be the overwhelming majority of society whereas a dictatorship can only be wielded by a minority.) The private, profit-making capitalism that is the root of all social problems has now been eliminated and this, most obscurely, causes the new government to disappear, leaving behind a classless, egalitarian society.

This is not the place to give a detailed account of what is wrong with Karl Marx's philosophy. What is relevant to the present purpose is that Russia was quite the wrong country for the revolution Marx had forecast. Far from being the advanced industrial country of Marx's prescription, Russia was an industrially backward, largely peasant country. According to Marxist theory, then, Russia had to first pass through a bourgeois revolution which would industrialise the country before it could have the proletarian revolution which would abolish capitalism. Another Marxist party, the Mensheviks, stuck to this rigid Marxist formula but the Bolsheviks, headed by Lenin, treated their proclaimed Marxism more lightly.

The central tenet of Marxism is to bring the means of production under control of central government and what had happened in Russia was something radically different from this - the dissolution of central government. The peasants and workers had taken charge of their own lives and were running the economic activity of the country through elected councils which they called soviets. The slogan that had inspired the Russian people was not the 'all power to the central government' of Marxism but 'all power to the soviets'. So when Lenin adopted the popular slogan this was a second defiance of his Marxism. He had to persuade a puzzled Bolshevik party to follow him in this deceitful and successful ploy to win popular support. As events soon showed, Lenin's enthusiasm for the soviets was solely tactical, read dishonest, and was jettisoned as soon as possible.

Another example of Bolshevik unprincipledness concerns Russia's post-revolution parliament, the Constituent Assembly. The Bolsheviks supposedly believed in parliamentary democracy since they participated in the elections but their belief did not extend to accepting the result of an election they had lost. Unsurprisingly in an overwhelmingly peasant country the elections were won by a party, the Socialist Revolutionists, which based its support on the peasantry, rather than one like the Bolsheviks which relied on the much smaller industrial working class. In early 1918 the Constituent Assembly was dissolved by force.

In the meantime there were various attempts to restore the Tsar's regime. The Bolsheviks, and many others, fought the White Russians and eventually the Tsar's supporters were beaten. But whilst fighting off one counter-revolution the Bolsheviks had carried out their own. The independence of the soviets and labour unions had been destroyed. Food was taken from the peasants by force and in the factories the elected soviets were replaced by managers from the Tsarist period. This was the centralisation of Marx's prescription and it was enforced by a terroristic secret police, the Cheka, accountable only to the leaders of the Bolsheviks. There were peasant rebellions and workers' strikes against the new order and in March 1921 there was a revolt at the naval fortress of Kronstadt. The Bolsheviks claimed that the revolt was an attempt to restore the old dictatorship but the truth is that it was an attempt to get rid of the new one. The demands of the insurgent sailors, given later, show what sort of society the sailors were fighting for and thus what sort of society the Bolsheviks had imposed. For example, when the sailors demanded freedom of speech and press for workers and peasants this was because that freedom no longer existed in Bolshevik Russia.

After over a week of fighting the sailors were beaten and Bolshevik tyranny re-established. But peasant rebellions were now too widespread to be suppressed even by the terrorist methods of the Cheka and so, immediately after Kronstadt, Lenin performed another political back somersault. He again abandoned his Marxism. The forced requisitions that had pushed the peasants to revolt were denounced as War Communism, though they were orthodox Marxism, and a partial restoration of capitalism, the New Economic Policy, was announced. This was the capitalism which the Bolsheviks had always denounced but which was more acceptable to the Russian people than the new Bolshevik society. Relaxing their dictatorship allowed the Bolsheviks to continue it. As Alexander Berkman asks, were Lenin and the Bolsheviks interested in anything other than their own power?

Berkman is a valuable eye-witness to the Bolshevik political revolution that destroyed Russia's social revolution. His personal history, prior to his arrival in revolutionary Russia, shows his commitment to social revolution. He was born in Russia in 1870 but emigrated to the United States in 1888 where in 1892 he was jailed for trying to kill an industrialist during a strike. His subsequent 14 years in prison are recorded in his *Prison Memoirs of an Anarchist*, a personal document of unusual power. On release he resumed his activities and was later jailed for 2 years for opposing the involvement of the United States in the First World War. After his release from this imprisonment he and others, including Emma Goldman, were deported to Russia. Berkman records in *The Russian Tragedy* the quasi-religious feeling he had on reaching a country where social revolution had occurred. So it is not possible to dismiss Berkman's account of what he saw as the prejudiced view of someone who was against the Bolsheviks from the start. On the contrary, despite his anarchism he was slow to admit to himself the truth about Russia - that the Bolsheviks had destroyed the social revolution. It was only after Kronstadt that Berkman allowed his illusions to be dispelled and at the end of that year, 1921, he, Goldman and Alexander Shapiro left Russia.

Once out of Russia Berkman started to spread the news about what was happening there. The 3 pamphlets collected here were all published in 1922 and are obviously contemporary accounts written by eye-witnesses. With hindsight we know that there was no third revolution that restored the gains of the original social revolution. Instead the Bolshevik (now Communist) dictatorship strengthened its hold on Russia until Lenin's eventual successor, Stalin, was able to re-impose the Marxist programme of state control of the means of production, thus reversing the defeat of the New Economic Policy. The horror of Stalin's enforced collectivisation and its consequences is well known. It now seems strange to find Berkman and others using the word communism (with a lower case c) in its original meaning. We are now far more used to thinking of Communism (with an upper case c) to denote societies like present day Russia.

Russia is a large, powerful state which combines internal repression with external aggression. The Marxists achieved their goal of state control of the means of production and it was a disaster. Despite the abolition of private capitalism the state has not shown the slightest sign of withering away (in Friedrich Engels' phrase) but whoever seriously supposed that it would? The Bolsheviks' aim was power, just as Karl Marx's had been before them, and they achieved it by a combination of terrorism and lack of principle. The dictatorship of the proletariat proved to be dictatorship over the proletariat and over everyone else as well. That for so long so many people were fooled into believing that Bolshevik tyranny was a desirable alternative to the West is a great irony and tragedy. Those of us who have seen through the fraud of parliamentary democracy must look elsewhere than Russia for an alternative since all the Bolsheviks have shown us is how to establish a society worse than the one we protest against.

The text of this book is based on that of the Cienfuegos Press edition of 1976 where the 3 original pamphlets were first published together in one volume. To keep the price of the book down the photographs in the Cienfuegos Press edition have been omitted, as have Berkman's preface to the pamphlet *The Russian Tragedy* and his foreword to the pamphlet *The Russian Revolution and the Communist Party*. William G. Nowlin's introduction to the Cienfuegos Press edition has also been omitted (and is replaced by a shorter one). Berkman wrote *The Russian Tragedy* and *The Kronstadt Rebellion* and translated *The Russian Revolution and the Communist Party*. As he records in the foreword omitted here *The Russian Revolution and the Communist Party* was 'the joint work of 4 well known Moscow Anarchists. Their names cannot be mentioned at present, in view of the fact that some of them are still in Russia'. Berkman's original plan was for a long series of pamphlets but it didn't work out and only 3 appeared. Instead he helped Emma Goldman prepare her *My Disillusionment in Russia* and later wrote his own *The Bolshevik Myth*. He held his anarchist views up to his death (by suicide) in June 1936 and he also wrote a contribution to anarchist theory, *What Is Communist Anarchism?*

The Russian Tragedy

1

It is most surprising how little is known, outside of Russia, about the actual situation and the conditions prevailing in that country. Even intelligent persons, especially among the workers, have the most confused ideas about the character of the Russian Revolution, its development, and its present political, economic and social status. Understanding of Russia and of what has been happening there since 1917 is most inadequate, to say the least. Though the great majority of people side either with or against the Revolution, speak for or against the Bolsheviks, yet almost nowhere is there concrete knowledge and clarity in regard to the vital subjects involved. Generally speaking, the views expressed - friendly or otherwise - are based on very incomplete and unreliable, frequently entirely false, information about the Russian Revolution, its history and the present phase of the Bolshevik regime. But not are the opinions entertained founded, as a rule, on insufficient or wrong data; too often they are deeply coloured - properly speaking, distorted - by partisan feeling, personal prejudice, and class interests. On the whole, it is sheer ignorance, in one form or another, which characterises the attitude of the great majority of people towards Russia and Russian events.

And yet, understanding of the Russian situation is most vital to the future progress and well-being of the world. On the correct estimation of the Russian Revolution, the role played in it by the Bolsheviks and by other political parties and movements, and the causes that have brought about the present situation, - in short, on a thorough conception of the whole problem depends what lessons we shall draw from the great historic events of 1917. Those lessons will, for good or evil, affect the opinions and the activities of great masses of mankind. In other words, coming social changes - and the labour and revolutionary efforts preceding and accompanying them - will be profoundly, essentially influenced by the popular understanding of what has really happened in Russia.

It is generally admitted that the Russian Revolution is the most important historic event since the Great French Revolution. I am even inclined to think that, in point of its potential consequences, the Revolution of 1917 is the most significant fact in the whole known history of mankind. It is the only Revolution which aimed, *de facto*, at social world-revolution; it is the only one which actually abolished the capitalist system on a country- wide scale, and fundamentally altered all social relationships existing till then. An event of such human and historic magnitude must not by judged from the narrow viewpoint of partisanship. No subjective feeling or preconception should be consciously permitted to colour one's attitude. Above all, every phase of the Revolution must be carefully studied, without bias or prejudice, and all the facts dispassionately considered, to enable us to form a just and adequate opinion. I believe - I am firmly convinced - that only **the whole truth** about Russia, irrespective of any considerations whatever, can be of ultimate benefit.

Unfortunately, such has not been the case so far, as a general rule. It was natural, of course, for the Russian Revolution to arose bitterest antagonism, on the one hand, and most passionate defence, on the other. But partisanship, of whatever camp, is not an objective judge. To speak plainly, the most atrocious lies, as well as ridiculous fairy tales, have been spread about Russia, and are continuing to be spread, even at this late day. Naturally it is not to be wondered at that the enemies of the Russian Revolution, the enemies of revolution as such, the reactionaries and their tools, should have flooded the world with most venomous misrepresentation of events transpiring in Russia. About them and their 'information' I need not waste any further words : in the eyes of honest, intelligent people they are discredited long ago.

But, sad to state, it is the would-be friends of Russia and of the Russian Revolution who have done the greatest harm to the Revolution, to the Russian people, and to the best interests of the working masses of the world, by their exercise of zeal untempered by truth. Some unconsciously, but most of them consciously and intentionally, have been lying, persistently and cheerfully, in defiance of all facts, in the mistaken notion that they are 'helping the Revolution'. Reasons of 'political expediency', of 'Bolshevik diplomacy', of the alleged 'necessity of the hour', and frequently motives of less unselfish considerations, have actuated them. The sole decent consideration of decent men, of real friends of the Russian Revolution and of man's emancipation - as well as of reliable history, - **consideration for truth,** they have entirely ignored.

There have been honourable exceptions, unfortunately too few : their voice has almost been lost in the wilderness of misrepresentation, falsehood, and overstatement. But most of those who visited Russia simply lied about the conditions in that country, - I repeat it deliberately. Some lied because they did not know any better : they had had neither the time nor the opportunity to study the situation, to learn the facts. They made 'flying trips', spending ten days or a few weeks in Petrograd or Moscow, unfamiliar with the language, never for a moment coming in direct touch with the real life of the people, hearing and seeing only what was told or shown them by the interested officials accompanying them at every step. In many cases these 'students of the Revolution' were veritable innocents abroad, naive to the point of the ludicrous. So unfamiliar were they with the environment, that in most cases they had not even the faintest suspicion that their affable 'interpreter', so eager to 'show and explain everything', was in reality a member of the 'trusted men', specially assigned to 'guide' important visitors. Many such visitors have since spoken and written voluminously about the Russian Revolution, with little knowledge and less understanding.

Others there were who had the time and the opportunity, and some of them really tried to study the situation seriously, not merely for the purpose of journalistic 'copy'. During my two years' stay in Russia I had occasion to come in personal contact with almost every foreign visitor, with the Labour missions, and with practically every delegate from Europe, Asia, America and Australia, who gathered in Moscow to attend the International Communist Congress held there last year.(1921.) Most of them could see and understand what was happening in the country. But it was a rare exception, indeed, that had vision and courage enough to realise that only the whole truth could serve the best interests of the situation.

As a general rule, however, the various visitors to Russia were extremely careless of the truth, systematically so, the moment they began 'enlightening' the world. Their assertions frequently bordered on criminal idiocy. Think, for instance, of George Lansbury (publisher of the London *Daily Herald*) stating that the ideas of brotherhood, equality, and love preached by Jesus the Nazerene were being realised in Russia - and that at the very time when Lenin was deploring the 'necessity of **military** communism forced upon us by Allied intervention and blockade'. Consider the 'equality' that divided the population of Russia into 36 categories, according to the ration and wages received. Another Englishman, a noted writer, emphatically claimed that everything would be well in Russia, were it not for outside interference - while whole districts in the East, the South, and in Siberia, some of them larger in area than France, were in armed rebellion against the Bolsheviks and their agrarian policy. Other literati were extolling the 'free Soviet system' of Russia, while 18,000 of her sons lay dead at Kronstadt in the struggle **to achieve** free Soviets.

But why enlarge upon this literary prostitution? The reader will easily recall to mind the legion of Ananiases who have been strenuously denying the very existence of the things that Lenin tried to explain as inevitable. I know that many delegates and others believed that the real Russian situation, if known abroad, might strengthen the hand of the reactionists and interventionists. Such a belief, however, did not necessitate the painting of Russia as a veritable labour Eldorado. But the time when it might have been considered inadvisable to speak fully of the Russian situation is long past. That period has been terminated, relegated into the archives of history, by the introduction of the 'new economic policy'. Now the time has come when we must learn the full lesson of the Revolution and the causes of its debacle. That we may avoid the mistakes it made (Lenin frankly says they were many), that we be enabled to adopt its best features, we must know the **whole truth** about Russia.

It is therefore that I consider the activities of certain labour men as positively criminal and a betrayal of the true interests of the workers of the world. I refer to the men and women, some of them delegates to the Congresses held in Moscow in 1921, that still continue to propagate the 'friendly' lies about Russia, delude the masses with roseate pictures of labour conditions in that country, and even seek to induce workers of other lands to migrate in large numbers to Russia. They are strengthening the appalling confusion already existing in the popular mind, deceive the proletariat by false statements of the present and vain promises for the near future. They are perpetuating the dangerous delusion that the Revolution is alive and continuously active in Russia. It is most despicable tactics. Of course, it is easy for an American labour leader, playing to the radical element, to write glowing reports about the condition of the Russian workingmen, while he is being entertained at State expense at the Luxe, the most lucrative hotel in Russia. Indeed, he may insist that 'no money is needed', for does **he** not receive everything his heart desires, free of charge? Or why should the President of an American needleworkers' union not state the Russian workers enjoy full liberty of speech? He is careful not to mention that only Communists and 'trusties' were permitted within speaking distance while the distinguished visitor was 'investigating' conditions in the factories.

May history be merciful to them.

2

That the reader may form a just estimate of what I shall say further, I think it necessary to sketch briefly my mental attitude at the time of my arrival in Russia.

It was two years ago. A democratic government, 'the freest on earth', had deported me - together with 248 other politicals - from the country I had lived in over 30 years. I had protested emphatically against the moral wrong perpetrated by an alleged democracy in resorting to methods it had so vehemently condemned on the part of the Tsarist autocracy. I branded deportation of politicals as an outrage on the most fundamental rights of man, and I fought it as a matter of principle.

But my heart was glad. Already at the outbreak of the February Revolution I had yearned to go to Russia. But the Mooney case had detained me : I was loath to desert the fight. Then I myself was taken prisoner by the United States, and penalised for my opposition to world slaughter. During 2 years the enforced hospitality of the Federal penitentiary at Atlanta, Georgia, prevented my departure. Deportation followed.

My heart was glad, did I say? Weak word to express the passion of joy that filled me at the certainty of visiting Russia. Russia! I was going to the country that had swept Tsardom off the map, I was to behold the land of the Social Revolution! Could there be greater joy to one who in his very childhood had been a rebel against tyranny, whose youth's unformed dreams had visioned human brotherhood and happiness, whose entire life was devoted to the Social Revolution?!

The journey was an inspiration. Though we were prisoners, treated with military severity, and the *Buford* a leaky old tub repeatedly endangering our lives during the month's Odyssey, yet the thought that we were on the way to the land of revolutionary promise kept the whole company of deportees in high spirits, atremble with expectation of the great Day soon to come. Long, long was the voyage,

RT-B

shameful the conditions we were forced to endure :crowded below
deck, living in constant wetness and foul air, fed on the poorest rations. Our patience was nigh exhausted, yet our courage unflagging,
and at last we reached our destination.

It was the 19th of January, 1920, when we touched the soil of
Soviet Russia. A feeling of solemnity, of awe, almost overwhelmed
me. Thus must have felt my pious old forefathers on first entering
the Holy of Holies. A strong desire was on me to kneel down and kiss
the ground - the ground consecrated by the life-blood of generations
of suffering and martyrdom, consecrated anew by the triumphant
revolutionists of my own day. Never before, not even when released
from the horrible nightmare of 14 years prison, had I been stirred so
profoundly, - longing to embrace humanity, to lay my heart at its
feet, to give my life a 1,000 times, were it but possible, to the service
of the Social Revolution. It was the most sublime day of my life.

We were received with open arms. The revoltionary hymn, played
by the military Red Band, greeted us enthusiastically as we crossed
the Russian frontier. The hurrahs of the red-capped defenders of the
Revolution echoed through the woods, rolling into the distance like
threats of thunder. With bowed head I stood in the presence of the
visible symbols of the Revolution Triumphant. With bowed head and
bowed heart. My spirit was proud, yet meek with the consciousness
of **actual** Social Revolution. What depths, what grandeur lay therein,
what incalcuable possibilities stretched in its vistas!

I heard the still voice of my soul : 'May your past life have contributed, if ever so little, to the realisation of the great human ideal, to
this, its successful beginning'. And I became conscious of the great
happiness it offered me; to do, to work, to help with every fibre of
my being the complete revolutionary expression of this wonderful
people. They had fought and won. They proclaimed the Social Revolution. It meant that oppression had ceased, that submission and
slavery, man's twin curses, were abolished. The hope of generations,
of ages, has at last been realised; justice has been established on the
earth - at least on that part of it that was Soviet Russia, and never-
more shall the precious heritage be lost.

But years of war and revolution have exhausted the country. There
is suffering and hunger, and much need of stout hearts and willing
hands to do and help. My heart sang for joy. Aye, I will give mvself
fully, completely, to the service of the people; I shall be rejuvenated
and grow young again in ever greater effort, in the hardest toil, for
for the furtherance of the common weal. My very life will I consecrate
to the realisation of the world's greatest hope, the Social Revolution.

At the first Russian army outpost a mass meeting was held to welcome us. The large hall crowded with soldiers and sailors, the nun-dressed women on the speaker's platform, their speeches, the whole atmosphere palpitating with Revolution in action, - all made a deep impression on me. Urged to say something, I thanked the Russian comrades for their warm welcome of the American deportees, congratulated them on their heroic struggle, and expressed my great joy at being in their midst. And then my whole thought and feeling fused in one sentence. 'Dear Comrades', I said, 'we came not to teach but to learn; to learn and to help'.

Thus I entered Russia. Thus felt my fellow-deportees.

I remained two years. What I learned, I learned gradually, day by day, in various parts of the country. I had exceptional opportunities for observation and study. I stood close to the leaders of the Communist Party, associated much with the most active men and women, participated in their work, and travelled extensively through the country under conditions most favourable to personal contact with the life of the workers and peasants. At first I could not believe that what I saw was real. I would not believe my eyes, my ears, my judgement. As those trick mirrors that make you appear dreadfully monstrous, so Russia seemed to reflect the Revolution as a frightful perversion. It was an appalling caricature of the new life, the world's hope. I shall not go into detailed description of my first impressions, my investigations, and the long process that resulted in my final conviction. I fought relentlessly, bitterly, against myself. For two years I fought. It is hardest to convince him who does not want to be convinced. And, I admit, I did not want to admit that the Revolution in Russia had become a mirage, a dangerous deception. Long and hard I struggled against this conviction. Yet proofs were accumulating, and each day brought more damning testimony. Against my will, against my hopes, against the holy fire of admiration and enthusiasm for Russia which burned within me, I was convinced - convinced that the Russian Revolution **had been done to death.**

How and by whom?

3

It has been asserted by some writers that Bolshevik accession to power in Russia was due to a *coup de main*, and doubt has been expressed regarding the social nature of the October change.

Nothing could be further from the truth. As a matter of historic fact, the great event known as the October Revolution was in the profoundest sense a **social** revolution. It was characterised by all the essentials of such a fundamental change. It was accomplished not by any political party, but by the people themselves, in a manner that radically transformed all the heretofore existing economic, political and social relations. But it did not take place in October. That month witnessed only the formal 'legal sanction' of the revolutionary events that had preceded it. For weeks and months prior to it the **actual** Revolution had been going on all over Russia; the city proletariat was taking possession of the shops and factories, while the peasants expropriated the big estates and turned the land to their own use. At the same time workers' committees, peasant committees and Soviets sprang up all over the country, and there began the gradual transfer of power from the provisional government to the Soviets. That took place, first in Petrograd, then in Moscow, and quickly spread to the Volga region, the Ural district, and to Siberia. The popular will found expression in the slogan, 'All power to the Soviets', and it went sweeping through the length and breadth of the land. The people had risen, the **actual** Revolution was on. The keynote of the situation was struck by the Congress of the Soviets of the North, proclaiming, 'The provisional government of Kerensky must go; the Soviets are the sole power!

That was on October 10th. Practically all the real power was already with the Soviets. In July the Petrograd rising against Kerensky was crushed, but in August the influence of the revolutionary workers and of the garrison was strong enough to enable them to prevent the attack planned by Korniloff. The Petrograd Soviet gained strength from day to day. On October 16th it organised its own Revolutionary Military Committee, an act of defiance of and open challenge to the government. The Soviet, through its Revolutionary Military Committee, prepared to defend Petrograd against the coalition government of Kerensky and the possible attack of General Kaledin and his counter-revolutionary cossacks. On October 22nd the whole proletarian population of Petrograd, solidarically supported by the garrison, demonstrated throughout the city against the government and in favour of 'All power to the Soviets'.

The All-Russian Congress of Soviets was to open October 25th. The provisional government, knowing its very existence in imminent peril, resorted to drastic action. On October 23rd the Petrograd Soviet ordered the Kerensky cabinet to withdraw within 48 hours. Driven to desperation, Kerensky undertook - on October 24th - to suppress the revolutionary press, arrest the most prominent revolutionists of Petrograd, and remove the active Commissars of the Soviet. The government relied on the 'faithful' troops and in the young *junkers* of the military student schools. But it was too late; the attempt to sustain the government failed. During the night of October 24th - 25th (November 6th - 7th) the Kerensky government was dissolved - peacefully, without bloodshed - and the exclusive supremacy of the Soviets was established. The Communist Party stepped into power. It was the political culmination of the Russian Revolution.

4

Various factors contributed to the success of the Revolution. To begin with, it met with almost no active opposition; the Russian bourgeoisie was unorganised, weak, and not of a militant disposition. But the main reasons lay in the all-absorbing enthusiasm with which the revolutionary slogans had fired the whole people. 'Down with the war!' , 'Immediate peace!', 'The land to the peasant, the factory to the workers!', 'All power to the Soviets!' - these were expressive of the passionate soul cry and deepest needs of the great masses. No power could withstand their miraculous effect.

Another very potent factor was the unity of the various revolutionary elements in their opposition to the Kerensky government. Bolsheviks, Anarchists, the left faction of the Social - Revolutionary party, the numerous politicals freed from prison and Siberian exile, and the hundreds of returned revolutionary emigrants, had all worked during the February - October months toward a common goal.

But if 'it was easy to begin' the Revolution, as Lenin had said in one of his speeches, to develop it, to carry it to its logical conclusion was another and more difficult matter. Two conditions were essential to such a consumation; continued unity of all the revolutionary forces, and the application of the country's good-will, initiative and best energies to the important work of the new social construction. It must always be remembered - and remembered well - that revolution does not mean destruction only. It means destruction **plus** construction, with the greatest emphasis on the plus. Most unfortunately, Bolshevik principles and methods were soon fated to prove a handicap, a drawback upon the creative activities of the masses.

The Bolsheviks are Marxists. Though in the October days they had accepted and proclaimed anarchist watchwords (direct action by the people, expropriation, free Soviets, and so forth), it was not their social philosophy that dictated this attitude. They had felt the popular pulse - the rising waves of the Revolution had carried them far beyond their theories. But they remained Marxists. At heart they had no faith in the people and their creative initiative. As social democrats they distrusted the peasantry, counting rather upon the support of the small revolutionary minority among the industrial element. They had advocated the Constituent Assembly, and only when they were convinced that they would not have a majority there, and therefore not be able to take State power into their own hands, they suddenly decided upon the dissolution of the Assembly, though the step was a refutation and a denial of fundamental Marxist principles. (Incidentally, it was an Anarchist, Anatoly Zheleznyakov, in charge of the palace guard, who took the initiative in the matter). As Marxists, the Bolsheviks insisted on the nationalisation of the land; ownership, distribution and control to be in the hands of the State. They were in principle opposed to socialisation, and only the pressure of the left faction of the Social Revolutionists (the Spiridonova-Kamkov) wing) whose influence among the peasantry was traditional, forced the Bolsheviks to 'swallow the agrarian programme of the Social Revolutionists whole', as Lenin afterwards put it.

From the first days of their accession to political power the Marxist tendencies of the Bolsheviks began to manifest themselves, to the detriment of the Revolution. Social Democratic distrust of the peasantry influenced their methods and measures. At the All-Russian Conferences the peasants did not receive equal representation with the industrial workers. Not only the village speculator and exploiter, but the agrarian population as a whole was branded by the Bolsheviks as 'petty bosses' and 'bourgeois', 'unable to keep step with the proletariat on the road to socialism'. The Bolshevik government discriminated against the peasant representatives in the Soviets and at the National Conferences, sought to handicap their independent efforts, and systematically narrowed the scope and activities of the Land Commissariat, then by far the most vital factor in the reconstruction of Russia. (The Commissariat was then presided over by a Left Social Revolutionist.) Inevitably this attitude lead to much dissatisfaction on the part of the great peasant masses. The Russian *muzhik* is simple and naive, but with the instinct of the primitive man he quickly senses a wrong; no fine dialectics can budge his once settled conviction. The very cornerstone of the Marxist credo, the dictatorship of the proletariat, served as an affront and an injury to the peasantry. They demanded an equal share in the organisation and administration of the country. Had they not been enslaved, oppressed and ignored long enough? The dictatorship of the proletariat the peasant resented as discrimination against himself. 'If dictatorship must be', he argued, 'why not of **all** who labour, of the town worker and of the peasant, together?'

Then came the Brest-Litovsk peace. In its far-reaching results it proved the death blow to the Revolution. Two months previously, in December, 1917, Trotsky had refused, with a fine gesture of noble indignation, the peace offered by Germany on conditions much more favourable to Russia. 'We wage no war, we sign no peace!', he had said, and revolutionary Russia applauded him. 'No compromise with German imperialism, no concessions', echoed through the length and breadth of the country, and the people stood ready to defend their Revolution to the very death. But now Lenin demanded the ratification of a peace that meant the most mean-spirited betrayal of the greater part of Russia. Finland, Latvia, Lithuania, Ukraina, White Russia, Bessarabia - all were to be turned over to the oppression and exploitation of the German invader and of their own bourgeoisie. It was a monstrous thing - the sacrifice at once of the principles of the Revolution and of its interests as well.

Lenin insisted on ratification, on the ground that the Revolution needed a 'breathing spell', that Russia was exhausted, and that peace would enable the 'revolutionary oasis' to gather strength for new effort. Radek denounced acceptance of Brest-Litovsk conditions as betrayal of the October Revolution. Trotsky disagreed with Lenin. The revolutionary forces split. The Left Social Revolutionists, most of the Anarchists and many of the non-partisan revolutionary elements were bitterly opposed to making peace with imperialism, especially on the terms dictated then by Germany. They declared that such a peace would be fatal to the Revolution; that the principle of 'peace without annexations' must not be sacrificed; that the German conditions involved the basest treachery to the workers and peasants of the provinces demanded by the Prussians; that the peace would subject the whole of Russia to economic and political dependence upon German Imperialism, that the invaders would possess themselves of the Ukranian bread and the Don coal, and drive Russia to industrial ruin.

But Lenin's influence was potent. He prevailed. The Brest-Litovsk treaty was ratified by the 4th Soviet Congress.

It was Trotsky who first asserted, in refusing the German peace terms offered in December, 1917, that the workers and peasants, inspired and armed by the Revolution, could by guerilla warfare overcome any army of invasion. The Left Social Revolutionists now called for peasant uprisings to oppose the Germans, confident that no army could conquer the revolutionary ardour of a people fighting for the fruits of their great Revolution. Workers and peasants, responding to this call, formed military detachments and rushed to the aid of Ukraina and White Russia, then valiantly struggling against the German invaders. Trotsky ordered the Russian army to pursue and suppress these partisan units.

The killing of Mirbach followed. It was the protest of the Left Social Revolutionist Party against, and the defiance of, Prussian imperialism within Russia. The Bolshevik government initiated repressive measures; it now felt itself, as it were, under obligations to Germany. Dzerzhinsky, head of the All-Russian Extraordinary Commission, demanded the delivery of the terrorist. It was a situation unique in revolutionary annals; a revolutionary party in power demanding of another revolutionary party, with which it had till then co-operated, the arrest and punishment of a revolutionist for executing the representative of an imperialist government! The Brest-Litovsk peace had put the Bolsheviks in the anomalous position of a gendarme for the Kaiser. The Left Social Revolutionists responded to Dzerzhinsky's demand by arresting the latter. This act, and the armed skirmishes that followed it (though insignificant in themselves) were thoroughly exploited by the Bolsheviks politically. They declared that it was an attempt of the Left Social Revolutionist Party to seize the reins of government. They announced that party outlawed, and their extermination began.

These Bolshevik methods and tactics were not accidental. Soon it became evident that it is the settled policy of the Communist State to crush every form of expression not in accord with the government

After the ratification of the Brest-Litovsk peace the Left Social Revolutionist Party withdrew its representative in the Soviet of People's Commissars. The Bolsheviks thus remained in exclusive control of the government. Under one pretext and another there followed most arbitrary and cruel suppression of all the other political parties and movements. The Mensheviks and Right Social Revolutionists had been 'liquidated' long before, together with the Russian bourgeoisie. Now it was the turn of the revolutionary elements - the Left Social Revolutionists, the Anarchists, the non-partisan revolutionists.

But the 'liquidation' of these involved much more that the suppression of small political groups. These revolutionary elements had strong followings, the Left Social Revolutionists among the peasantry, the Anarchists mainly among the city proletariat. The new Bolshevik tactics encompassed systematic eradication of every sign of dissatisfaction, stifling all criticism and crushing independent opinion or effort. With this phase the Bolsheviks enter upon the dictatorship **over** the proletariat, as it is popularly characterised in Russia. The government's attitude to the peasantry is now that of open hostility. More increasingly is violence resorted to. Labour unions are dissolved, frequently by force, when their loyalty to the Communist Party is suspected. The co-operatives are attacked. This great organisation, the fraternal bond between city and country, whose economic functions were so vital to the interests of Russia and of the Revolution, is hindered in its important work of production, exchange and distribution of the necessaries of life, is disorganised, and finally completely abolished.

Arrests, night searches, *zassada* (house blockade), executions, are the order of the day. The Extraordinary Commissions (Cheka), originally organised to fight counter-revolution and speculation, is becoming the terror of every worker and peasant. Its secret agents are everywhere, always unearthing 'plots', signifying the *razstrel* (shooting) of hundreds without hearing, trial or appeal. From the intended defence of the Revolution the Cheka becomes the most dreaded organisation, whose injustice and cruelty spread terror over the whole country. All-powerful, owing no one responsibility, the Cheka is a law unto itself, possesses its own army, assumes police, judicial, administrative and executive powers, and makes its own laws that supercede those of the official State. The prisons and concentration camps are filled with alleged counter-revolutionists and speculators, 95 per cent of whom are starved workers, simple peasants, and even children of 10 to 14 years of age. (See reports of prison investigations, Petrograd *Krasnaya Gazetta* and *Pravda*; Moscow *Pravda*, May, June, July, 1920). Communism becomes synonymous in the popular mind with

Chekism, the latter the epitome of all that is vile and brutal. The seed of counter-revolutionary feeling is sown broadcast.

The other policies of the 'revolutionary government' keep step with these developments. Mechanical centralisation, run mad, is paralysing the industrial and economic activities of the country. Initiative is frowned upon, free effort systematically discouraged. The great masses are deprived of the opportunity to shape the policies of the Revolution, or take part in the administration of the affairs of the country. The government is monopolising every avenue of life; the Revolution is divorced from the people. A bureaucratic machine is created that is appalling in its parasitism, inefficiency and corruption. In Moscow alone this new class of *sovburs* (Soviet bureaucrats) exceeds, in 1920, the total of office holders throughout the whole of Russia under the Tsar in 1914. (See official report of investigation by Committee of Moscow Soviet, 1921). The Bolshevik economic policies, effectively aided by this bureaucracy, completely disorganise the already crippled industrial life of the country. Lenin, Zinoviev, and other Communist leaders thunder philippics against the new Soviet bourgeoisie, - and issue ever new decrees that strengthen and augment its numbers and influence.

The system of *yedinolitchiye* is introduced; management by **one** person. Lenin himself is its originator and chief advocate. Henceforth the shop and factory committees are to be abolished, stripped of all power. Every mill, mine, and factory, the railroads and all the other industries are to be managed by a single head, a 'specialist', - and the old Tsarist bourgeoisie is invited to step in. The former bankers, bourse operators, mill owners and factory bosses become the managers, in full control of the industries, with absolute power over the workers. They are vested with authority to hire, employ and discharge the 'hands', to give or deprive them of the *payok* (food ration), even to punish them and turn them over to the Cheka. The workers, who had fought and bled for the Revolution and were willing to suffer, freeze and starve in its defence, resent this unheard of imposition. They regard it as the worse betrayal. They refuse to be dominated by the very owners and foremen whom they had driven, in the days of the Revolution, out of the factories and who had been so lordly and brutal to them. They have no interest in **such** a reconstruction. The 'new system', heralded by Lenin as the saviour of the industries, results in the complete paralysis of the economic life of Russia, drives the workers *en masse* from the factories, and fills them with bitterness and hatred of everything 'socialistic'. The principles and tactics of Marxian mechanisation of the Revolution are sealing its doom.

The fanatical delusion that a little conspirative group, as it were, could achieve a fundamental social transformation proved the Frankenstein of the Bolsheviks. It led them to incredible depths of infamy and barbarism. The methods of such a theory, its inevitable means, are two-fold; decrees and terror. Neither of these did the Bolsheviks spare. As Bukharin, the foremost ideologue of the militant Communists, taught, terrorism is the method by which capitalistic human nature is to be transformed into fit Bolshevik citizenship. Freedom is 'a bourgeois prejudice' (Lenin's favourite expression), liberty of speech and of the press unnecessary, harmful. The central government is the depositary of all knowledge and wisdom. It will do everything. The sole duty of the citizen is obedience. The will of the State is supreme.

Stripped of fine phrases, intended mostly for Western consumption, this was and is the practical attitude of the Bolshevik government. This government, the **real** and **only** actual government of Russia, consists of five persons, members of the inner circle of the Central Committee of the Communist Party of Russia. These 'Big Five' are omnipotent. This group, in its true essence conspiratory, has been controlling the fortunes of Russia and of the Revolution since the Brest-Litovsk peace. What has happened in Russia since, has been in strict accord with the Bolshevik interpretation of Marxism. That Marxism, reflected through the Communist inner circle's megalamania of omniscience and omnipotence, has achieved the present debacle of Russia.

In consonance with their theory, the social fundamentals of the October Revolution have been deliberately destroyed. The ultimate object being a powerfully centralised State, with the Communist Party in absolute control, the popular initiative and the revolutionary creative forces of the masses had to be eliminated. The elective system was abolished, first in the army and navy, then in the industries. The Soviets of peasants and workers were castrated and turned into obedient Communist committees, with the dreaded sword of the Cheka ever hanging over them. The labour unions governmentalised, their proper activities suppressed, they were turned into mere transmitters of the orders of the State. Universal military service, coupled with the death penalty for conscientious objectors; enforced labour, with a vast officialdom for the apprehension and punishment of 'deserters'; agrarian and industrial conscription of the peasantry; military Communism in the cities and the system of requisitioning in the country, characterised by Radek as simply **grain plundering** (*International Press Correspondence*, English edition, volume 1, number 17); the suppression of workers' protests by the military; the crushing of peasant dissatisfaction with an iron hand, even to the extent of whipping the peasants and razing their villages with artillery - (in the Ural, Volga and Kuban districts, in Siberia and the Ukraina) - this characterised the attitude of the Communist State towards the people, this comprised the 'constructive social and economic policies' of the Bolsheviks.

Still the Russian peasants and workers, prizing the Revolution for which they had suffered so much, kept bravely fighting on numerous military fronts. They were defending the Revolution, as they thought. They starved, froze, and died by the thousands, in the fond hope that the terrible things the Communists did would soon cease. The Bolshevik horrors were, somehow - the simple Russian thought - the inevitable result of the powerful enemies 'from abroad' attacking their beloved country. But when the wars will at last be over - the people naively echoed the official press - the Bolsheviks will surely return to the revolutionary path they entered in October, 1917, the path the wars had forced them temporarily to forsake.

The masses hoped and - endured. And then, at last, the wars were ended. Russia drew an almost audible sigh of relief, relief palpitating with deep hope. It was the crucial moment; the great test had come. The soul of a nation was aquiver. To be or not to be? And then full realisation came. The people stood aghast. Repressions continued, even grew worse. The piratical *razvyorstka*, the punitive expeditions against the peasants, did not abate their murderous work. The Cheka were unearthing more 'conspiracies', executions were taking place as before. Terrorism was rampant. The new Bolshevik bourgeoisie lorded it over the workers and the peasants, official corruption was vast and open, huge food supplies were rotting through Bolshevik inefficiency and centralised State monopoly, - and the people were starving.

The Petrograd workers, always in the forefront of revolutionary effort, were the first to voice their dissatisfaction and protest. The Kronstadt sailors, upon investigation of the demands of the Petrograd proletariat, declared themselves solidaric with the workers. In their turn they announced their stand for free Soviets, Soviets free from Communist coercion, Soviets that should in reality represent the revolutionary masses and voice their needs. In the middle provinces of Russia, in the Ukraina, on the Caucasus, in Siberia, everywhere the people made known their wants, voiced their grievances, informed the government of their demands. The Bolshevik State replied with its usual argument; the Kronstadt sailors were decimated, the 'bandits' of Ukraina massacred, the 'rebels' of the East laid low with machine guns.

This done, Lenin announced at the 10th Congress of the Communist Party of Russia (March, 1921) that his former policies were all wrong. The *razvyorstka*, the requisition of food, was pure robbery. Military violence against the peasantry a 'serious mistake'. The workers must receive some consideration. The Soviet bureaucracy is corrupt and criminal, a huge parasite. 'The methods we have been using have failed'. The people, especially the rural population, are not yet up to the level of Communist principles. Private ownership must be re-introduced, free trade established. Henceforth the best Communist is he who can drive the best bargain. (Lenin's expression).

5

Back to capitalism!

The present situation in Russia is most anomalous. Economically it is a combination of State and private capitalism. Politically it remains the 'dictatorship of the proletariat' or, more correctly, the dictatorship of the inner circle of the Communist Party.

The peasantry has forced the Bolsheviks to make concessions to it. Forcible requisitioning is abolished. Its place has taken the tax in kind, a certain percentage of the peasant produce going to the government. Free trade has been legalised, and the farmer may now exchange or sell his surplus to the government, to the re-established co-operatives or on the open market. The new economic policy opens wide the door of exploitation. It sanctions the right of enrichment and of wealth accumulation. The farmer may now profit by his successful crops, rent more land, and exploit the labour of those peasants who have little land and no horses to work it with. The shortage of cattle and bad harvests in some parts of the country have created a new class of 'farm hands' who hire themselves out to the well to do peasant. The poor people migrate from those regions which are suffering from famine and swell the ranks of this class. The village capitalist is in the making.

The city worker in Russia today, under the new economic policy, is in exactly the same position as in any other capitalistic country. Free food distribution is abolished, except in a few industries operated by the government. The worker is paid wages, and must pay for his necessaries - as in any country. Most of the industries, in so far as they are active, have been let or leased to private persons. The small capitalist now has a free hand. He has a large field for his activities.

The farmer's surplus, the product of the industries, of the peasant trades, and of all the enterprises of private ownership, are subject to the ordinary processes of business, can be bought and sold. Competition within the retail trade leads to incorporation and to the accumulation of fortunes in the hands of individuals.

Developing city capitalism and village capitalism cannot long co-exist with 'dictatorship of the proletariat'. The unnatural alliance between the latter and foreign capitalism will in the near future prove another vital factor in the fate of Russia.

The Bolshevik government still strives to uphold the dangerous delusion that the 'revolution is progressing', that Russia is 'ruled by proletarian soviets', that the Communist Party and its State are identical with the people. It is still speaking in the name of the 'proletariat'. It is seeking to dupe the people with a new chimera. After a while - the Bolsheviks now pretend - when Russia shall have become industrially resurrected, through the achievements of our fast growing capitalism, the 'proletarian dictatorship' will also have grown strong, and we will return to nationalisation. The State will then systematically curtail and supplant the private industries and thus break the power of the meanwhile developed bourgeoisie.

'After a period of partial denationalisation a stronger nationalisation begins', says Preobrazhensky, Finance Commissar, in his recent article, 'The Perspectives of the New Economic Policy'. Then will 'Socialism be victorious on the entire front' (*ibid*). Radek is less diplomatic. 'We certainly do not mean', he assures us in his political analysis of the Russian situation, entitled 'Is the Russian Revolution a Bourgeois Revolution?' (*International Press Correspondence*, 16th December, 1921) 'that at the end of a year we shall again confiscate the newly accumulated goods. Our economic policy is based upon a longer period of time....We are consciously preparing ourselves for co-operating with the bourgeoisie; this is undoubtedly dangerous to the existence of the Soviet government, because the latter loses the monopoly on industrial production as against the peasantry. Does not this signify the decisive victory of capitalism? May we not then speak of our revolution as having lost its revolutionary character?....'

To these very timely and significant questions Radek cheerfully answers with a categoric No! It is true, of course, as Marx taught, he admits, that economic relations determine the political ones, and that economic concessions to the bourgeoisie must lead also to political concessions. He remembers that when the powerful landowning class of Russia began making economic concessions to the bourgeoisie, those concessions were soon followed by political ones and finally by the capitulation of the landowning class. But he insists that the

Bolsheviks will retain their power even under the conditions of the restoration of capitalism. 'The bourgeoisie is a historically deteriorating, dying class....That is why the working class (?) of Russia can refuse to make political concessions to the bourgeoisie; since it is justified in hoping that its power will grow on a national and international scale more quickly than will the power of the Russian bourgeoisie'.

Meanwhile, though authoritatively assured that his 'power is to grow on a national and international scale', the Russian worker is in a bad plight. The new economic policy has made the proletarian 'dictator' a common, everyday wage slave, like his brother in countries unblessed with Socialist dictatorship. The curtailment of the government's national monopoly has resulted in the throwing of hundreds of thousands of men and women out of work. Many Soviet institutions have been closed; the remaining ones have discharged from 50 to 75 per cent of their employees. The large influx to the cities of peasants and villagers ruined by the *razvyorstka*, and those fleeing from the famine districts, has produced an unemployment problem of threatening scope. The revival of the industrial life through private capital is a very slow process, due to the general lack of confidence in the Bolshevik State and its promises.

But when the industries will again begin to function more or less systematically, Russia will face a very difficult and complex labour situation. Labour organisations, trade unions, do not exist in Russia, so far as the legitimate activities of such bodies are concerned. The Bolsheviks abolished them long ago. With developing production and capitalism, governmental as well as private, Russia will see the rise of a new proletariat whose interests must naturally come into conflict with those of the employing class. A bitter struggle is imminent. A struggle of a two-fold nature; against the private capitalist, and against the State as an employer of labour. It is even probable that the situation may develop still another phase; antagonism of the workers employed in the State-owned industries toward the better-paid workers of private concerns. What will be the attitude of the Bolshevik government? The object of the new economic policy is to encourage, in every way possible, the development of private enterprise and to accelerate the growth of industrialism. Shops, mines, factories and mills have already been leased to capitalists. Labour demands have a tendency to curtail profits; they interfere with the 'orderly processes' of business. And as for strikes, they handicap production, paralyse industry. Shall not the interests of Capital and Labour be declared solidaric in Bolshevik Russia?

The industrial and agrarian exploitation of Russia, under the new economic policy, must inevitably lead to the growth of a powerful labour movement. The workers' organisations will unite and solidify the city proletariat with the agrarian poor, in the common demand for better living conditions. From the present temper of the Russian worker, now enriched by his 4 years experience of the Bolshevik regime, it may be assumed with considerable degree of probability that the coming labour movement of Russia will develop along syndicalist lines. This sentiment is strong among the Russian workers. The principles and methods of revolutionary syndicalism are not unfamiliar to them. The effective work of the factory and shop committees, the first to initiate the industrial expropriation of the bourgeoisie in 1917, is an inspiring memory still fresh in the minds of the proletariat. Even in the Communist Party itself, among its labour elements, the syndicalist idea is popular. The famous Labour Opposition, led by Shliapnikov and Madame Kolontai within the party, is essentially syndicalistic.

What attitude will the Bolshevik government take to the labour movement about to develop in Russia, be it wholly or even only partly syndicalistic? Till now the State has been the mortal enemy of labour syndicalism **within** Russia, though encouraging it in other countries. At the 10th Congress of the Russian Communist Party (March, 1921) Lenin declared merciless warfare against the faintest sympton of syndicalist tendencies, and even the discussion of syndicalist theories was forbidden the Communists, on pain of exclusion from the Party. (See official report, 10th Congress). A number of the Labour Opposition were arrested and imprisoned. It is not to be lightly assumed that the Communist dictatorship could satisfactorily solve the difficult problems arising out of a real labour movement under Bolshevik autocracy. They involve principles of Marxian centralisation, the functioning of trade or industrial unions independent of the omnipotent government, and active opposition to private capitalism. But not only the big and small capitalist will the workers of Russia soon have to fight. They will presently come to grips with State capitalism itself.

To correctly understand the spirit and character of the present Bolshevik phase, it is necessary to realise that the so-called 'new economic policy' is neither new nor economic, properly considered. It is old political Marxism, the exclusive fountainhead of Bolshevik wisdom. As social democrats they have remained faithful to their bible. Only a country where capitalism is most highly developed can have a social revolution - that is the acme of Marxist faith. The Bolsheviks are about to apply it to Russia. True, in the October days of the Revolution they repeatedly deviated from the straight and narrow path of Marx. Not because they doubted the prophet. By no means. Rather that Lenin and his group, political opportunists, had been forced by irresistable popular aspiration to steer a truly revolutionary course. But all the time they hung onto the skirts of Marx, and sought every opportunity to direct the Revolution into Marxian channels. As Radek naively reminds us, 'already in April, 1918, in a speech by comrade Lenin, the Soviet government attempted to define our next tasks and to **point out the way which we now designate as the new economic policy**'. (*International Press Correspondence*, volume 1, number 17).

Significant admission! In truth, present Bolshevik policies are the continuation of the good orthodox Bolshevik Marxism of 1918. Bolshevik leaders now admit that the Revolution, in its post-October developments, was only political, not social. The mechanical centralisation of the Communist State - it must be emphasised - proved fatal to the economic and social life of the country. Violent party dictatorship destroyed the unity of the workers and the peasants, and created a perverted, bureaucratic attitude to revolutionary reconstruction. The complete denial of free speech and criticism, not only to the masses but even to the rank and file of the Communist Party itself, resulted in its undoing, **through its own mistakes.**

And now? Bolshevik Marxism is continuing in poor Russia. But it is monstrously criminal to prolong this bloody Comedy of Errors. Communist construction is not possible alongside of a sickly capitalism, artificially developed. That capitalism can never be destroyed - as Lenin and company pretend to believe - by the regular processes of the Bolshevik State grown economically strong. The 'new' policies are therefore a delusion and a snare, fundamentally reactionary. These policies themselves create the necessity for another revolution.

Must tortured humanity ever tread the same vicious circle?

Or will the workers at last learn the great lesson of the Russian Revolution that every government, whatever its fine name and nice promises, is by its inherent nature, as a government, destructive of the very purposes of the social revolution? It is the mission of government to govern, to subject, to strengthen and perpetuate itself. It is high time the workers learn that only their own organised, creative efforts, free from political and State interference, can make their age-long struggle for emancipation a lasting success.

RT-C

The Russian Revolution and
the Communist Party

The October Revolution was not the legitimate offspring of traditional Marxism. Russia but little resembled a country in which, according to Marx, 'the concentration of the means of production and the socialisation of the tools of labour reached the point where they can no longer be contained within their capitalist shell. The shell bursts....'

In Russia, 'the shell' burst unexpectedly. It burst at a stage of low technical and industrial development, when centralisation of the means of production had made little progress. Russia was a country with a badly organised system of transportation, with a weak bourgeoisie and weak proletariat, but with a numerically strong and socially important peasant population. In short, it was a country in which, apparently, there could be no talk of irreconcilable antagonism between the grown industrial labour forces and a fully ripened capitalist system.

But the combination of circumstances in Russia in 1917 involved, particularly for Russia, an exceptional state of affairs which resulted in the catastrophic breakdown of her whole industrial system. 'It was easy for Russia', Lenin justly wrote at the time, '**to begin** the socialist revolution in the peculiarly unique situation of 1917'.

The specially favourable conditions for the **beginning** of the socialist revolution were -

1) the possibility of blending the slogans of the Social Revolution with the popular demand for the termination of the imperialistic world war, which had produced great exhaustion and dissatisfaction among the masses.

2) the possibility of remaining, at least for a certain period after quitting the war, outside the sphere of influence of the capitalistic

European groups that continued the world war.

3) the opportunity to begin, even during the short time of this respite, the work of internal organisation and to prepare the foundation for revolutionary reconstruction.

4) the exceptionally favourable position of Russia, in case of possible new aggression of the part of West European imperialism, due to her vast territory and insufficient means of communication.

5) the advantages of such a condition in the event of civil war and

6) the possibility of almost immediately satisfying the fundamental demands of the revolutionary peasantry, notwithstanding the fact that the essentially democratic viewpoint of the agricultural population was entirely different from the socialist programme of the 'party of the proletariat' which seized the reins of government.

Moreover, revolutionary Russia already had the benefit of a great experience - the experience of 1905, when the Tsarist autocracy succeeded in crushing the revolution for the very reason that the latter strove to be exclusively political and therefore could neither arouse the peasants nor inspire even a considerable part of the proletariat.

The world war, by exposing the complete bankruptcy of constitutional government, served to prepare and quicken the greatest movement of the people - a movement which, by virtue of its very essence, could develop only into a social revolution.

Anticipating the measures of the revolutionary government, often even in defiance of the latter, the revolutionary masses by their own initiative began, long before the October days, to put in practice their social ideals. They took possession of the land, the factories, mines, mills, and the tools of production. They got rid of the more hated and dangerous representatives of government and authority. In their grand revolutionary outburst they destroyed every form of political and economic oppression. In the deeps of Russia the Social Revolution was raging, when the October change took place in the capitals of Petrograd and Moscow.

The Communist Party, which was aiming at the dictatorship, from the very beginning correctly judged the situation. Throwing overboard the democratic planks of its platform, it energetically proclaimed the slogans of the Social Revolution, in order to gain control of the movement of the masses. In the course of the development of the Revolution, the Bolsheviks gave concrete form to certain fundamental principles and methods of Anarchist Communism, as for instance; the negation of parliamentarism, expropriation of the bourgeoisie, tactics of direct action, seizure of the means of production, establishment of the system of Workers' and Peasants' Councils (Soviets), and so forth.

Furthermore, the Communist Party exploited all the popular de-

mands of the hour; termination of the war, all power to the revolutionary proletariat, the land for the peasants, etc. This, as we shall see
later, base demagoguery proved of tremendous psychological effect
in hastening and intensifying the revolutionary process.

But if it was easy, as Lenin said, **to begin** the Revolution, its further development and strengthening were to take place amid difficult
surroundings.

The **external** position of Russia, as characterised by Lenin about
the middle of 1918, continued to be 'unusually complicated and dangerous', and 'tempting for the neighbouring imperialist States by its
temporary weakness'. The Socialist Soviet Republic was in an 'extra-
ordinarily unstable, very critical international position.'

And, indeed, the whole subsequent external history of Russia is
full of difficulties in consequence of the necessity of fighting cease-
lessly, often on several fronts at once, against the agents of world imperialism, and even against common adventurers. Only after the final
defeat of the Wrangel forces was at last put an end to direct armed
interference in the affairs of Russia.

No less difficult and complex, even chaotic, was the **internal** situation of the country.

Complete breakdown of the whole industrial fabric; failure of the
national economy; disorganisation of the transportation system, hunger, unemployment; relative lack of organisation among the workers;
unusually complex and contradictory conditions of peasant life; the
psychology of the 'petty proprietor', inimical to the new Soviet regime; sabotage of Soviet work by the technical intelligentsia; the great
lack in the Party of trained workers familiar with local conditions,
and the practical inefficiency of the Party heads; finally, according
to the frank admission of the acknowledged leader of the Bolsheviks,
'the greatest hatred, by the masses, and distrust of everything governmental' - that was the situation in which the first and most difficult
steps of the Revolution had to be made.

It must also be mentioned that there were still other specific problems with which the revolutionary government had to deal. Namely,
the deep-seated contradictions and even antagonisms between the interests and aspirations of the various social groups of the country. The
most important of these were -

1) the most advanced, and in industrial centres the most influential,
group of factory proletarians. Notwithstanding their relative cultural
and technical backwardness, these elements favoured the application
of true communist methods.

2) the numerically powerful peasant population, whose economic
attitude was decisive, particularly at a time of industrial prostration

and blockade. This class looked with distrust and even hatred upon all attempts of the Communist government to play the guardian and control their economic activities.

3) the very large and psychologically influential group (in the sense of forming public opinion, even if of a panicky character) of the common citizenry; the residue of the upper bourgeoisie, technical specialists, small dealers, petty bosses, commercial agents of every kind - a numerous group, in which were also to be found functionaries of the old regime who adapted themselves and were serving the Soviet government, now and then sabotaging; elements tempted by the new order of things and seeking to make a career; and, finally, persons torn out of their habitual modes of life and literally starving. This class was approximately estimated at 70 per cent of the employees of Soviet institutions.

Naturally, each of these groups looked upon the Revolution with their own eyes, judged its further possibilities from their own point of view, and in their own peculiar manner reacted on the measures of the revolutionary government.

All these antagonisms, rending the country and frequently clashing in bloody strife, inevitably tended to nourish counter-revolution - not mere conspiracy or rebellion, but the terrific convulsion of a country experiencing two world cataclysms at once; war and social revolution.

Thus the political party that assumed the role of dictator was faced by problems of unprecedented difficulty. The Communist Party did not shrink from their solution, and in that is its immortal historic merit.

Notwithstanding the many deep antagonisms, in spite of the apparent absence of the conditions necessary for a social revolution, it was too late to discuss about driving back the uninvited guest, and await a new, more favourable opportunity. Only blind, dogmatic or positively reactionary elements could have imagined that the Revolution could have been 'made differently'. The Revolution was not and could be a mechanical product of the abstract human will. It was an organic process burst with elemental force from the very needs of the people, from the complex combination of circumstances that determined their existence.

To return to the old political and economical regime, that of industrial feudalism, was out of the question. It was impossible, and first of all because it were the denial of the greatest conquest of the Revolution; the right of every worker to a decent human life. It was also impossible because of the fundamental principles of the new national economy; the old regime was inherently inimical to the development of free social relationship - it had no room for labour initiative.

It was apparent that the only right and wholesome solution - which could save the Revolution from its external enemies, free it from the inner strife that rent the country, broaden and deepen the Revolution itself - lay in the direct, creative initiative of the toiling masses. Only they who had for centuries born the heaviest burdens could through conscious systematic effort find the road to a new, regenerated society. And that was to be the fitting culmination of their unexampled revolutionary zeal.

Lenin himself, replying in one of his works to the question, 'How is the discipline of the revolutionary party of the proletariat to be maintained, how to be strengthened?' clearly and definitely replied; 'By knowing how to meet, to combine, to some extent even to merge, if you will, with the broad masses of the toilers, mainly with the proletariat, but also **with the non-proletarian labouring masses**'. (Emphasis is Lenin's.)

However, this thought was and still remains, on the whole, in irreconcilable conflict with the spirit of Marxism in its official Bolshevik interpretation, and particularly with Lenin's authoritative view of it.

For years trained in their peculiar 'underground' social philosophy, in which fervent faith in the Social Revolution was in some odd manner blended with their no less fanatical faith in State centralisation, the Bolsheviks devised an entirely new science of tactics. It is to the effect that the preparation and consummation of the Social Revolution necessitates the organisation of a special conspirative staff, consisting exclusively of the theoreticians of the movement, vested with dictatorial powers for the purpose of clarifying and perfecting beforehand, by their own conspirative means, the class-consciousness of the proletariat.

Thus the fundamental characteristic of Bolshevik psychology was distrust of the masses, of the proletariat. Left to themselves, the masses - according to Bolshevik conviction - could rise only to the consciousness of the petty reformer.

The road that leads to the direct creativeness of the masses was thus forsaken.

According to Bolshevik conviction, the masses are 'dark', mentally crippled by ages of slavery. They are multi-coloured; besides the revolutionary advance-guard they comprise great numbers of the indifferent and many self-seekers. The masses, according to the old but still correct formula of Rousseau, must be made free by force. To educate them to liberty one must not hesitate to use compulsion and violence.

'Proletarian compulsion in all its forms', writes Bukharin, one of the foremost Communist theoreticians, 'beginning with summary execution and ending with compulsory labour is, however paradoxical

it may sound, a method of reworking the human material of the capitalist epoch into Communist humanity'.

This cynical doctrinairism, this fanatical quasi-philosophy flavour-
ed with Communist pedagogic sauce and aided by the pressure of
'canonised officials' (expression of the prominent Communist and
labour leader Shliapnikov) represent the actual methods of the Party
dictatorship, which retains the trademark of the 'dictatorship of the
proletariat' merely for gala affairs at home and for advertisement
abroad.

Already in the first days of the Revolution, early in 1918, when
Lenin first announced to the world his socio-economic programme
in its minutest details, the roles of the people and of the Party in the
revolutionary reconstruction were strictly separated and definitely
assigned. On the one hand, an absolutely submissive socialist herd, a
dumb people; on the other, the omniscient, all-controlling Political
Party. What is inscrutable to all, is an open book to It. In the land
there may be only **one** indisputable source of truth - the State. But
the Communist State is, in essence and practice, the dictatorship of
the Party only, or - more correctly - the dictatorship of its Central
Committee. Each and every citizen must be, first and foremost, the
servant of the State, its obedient functionary, unquestioningly executing the will of his master - if not as a matter of conscience, then
out of fear. All free initiative, of the individual as well as of the col-
lectivity, is eliminated from the vision of the State. The peoples'
Soviets are transformed into sections of the Ruling Party; the Soviet
institutions become soulless offices, mere transmitters of the will of
the centre to the periphery. All expressions of State activity must be
stamped with the approving seal of Communism as interpreted by
the faction in power. Everything else is considered superfluous, useless and dangerous.

This system of barrack absolutism, supported by bullet and bayonet, has subjugated every phase of life, stopping neither before the
destruction of the best cultural values, nor before the most stupend-
ous squandering of human life and energy.

By its declaration *L'etat, c'est moi*, the Bolshevik dictatorship has
assumed entire responsibility for the Revolution in all its historic
and ethical implications.

Having paralysed the constructive efforts of the people, the Communist Party could henceforth count only on its own initiative. By
what means, then, did the Bolshevik dictatorship expect to use to
best advantage the resources of the Social Revolution? What road

did it choose, not merely to subjugate the masses mechanically to its authority, but also to educate them, to inspire them with advanced socialist ideas, and to stimulate them - exhausted as they were by long war, economic ruin and police rule - with new faith in socialist reconstruction? What has it substituted in place of the revolutionary enthusiasm which burned so intensely before?

Two things, which comprised the beginning and the end of the constructive activities of the Bolshevik dictatorship;

1) the theory of the Communist State, and

2) terrorism.

In his speeches about the Communist programme, in discussions at conferences and congresses, and in his celebrated pamphlet on 'Infantile Sickness of "Leftism" in Communism', Lenin gradually shaped that peculiar doctrine of the Communist State which was fated to play the dominant role in the attitude of the Party and to determine all the subsequent steps of the Bolsheviks in the sphere of practical politics. It is the doctrine of a zigzag political road; of 'respites' and 'tributes', agreements and compromises, profitable retreats, advantageous withdrawals and surrenders - a truly classical theory of compromise.

Scorning the 'chuckling and giggling of the lackeys of the bourgeoisie', Lenin calls upon the labouring masses to 'steer down the wind', to retreat, to watch and wait, to go slowly, and so on. Not the fiery spirit of Communism, but sober commercialism which can successfully bargain for a few crumbs of socialism from the still unconquered bourgeoisie - that is the 'need of the hour'. To encourage and develop the virtues of the trader, the spirit of parsimony and profitable dealing; that is the first commandment to the 'regenerated' people.

In the pamphlet referred to, Lenin scouts all stereotyped morality and compares the tactics of his Party with those of a military commander, ignoring the gulf which divides them and their aims. All means are good that lead to victory. There are compromises and compromises. 'The whole history of Bolshevism before and after the October Revolution', Lenin sermonises the 'naive German left Communists' who are stifling in their own revolutionary fervour, 'is **replete** with instances of agreements and compromises with other parties, the bourgeoisie included'. To prove his assertion, Lenin enumerates in great detail various cases of bargaining with bourgeois parties, beginning with 1905 and up to the adoption by the Bolsheviks, at the time of the October Revolution, 'of the agrarian platform of the soc-revolutionists, *in toto*, without change'.

Compromise and bargaining, for which the Bolsheviks so unmercifully and justly denounced and stigmatised all the other factions of State Socialism, now become the Bethlehem Star pointing the way to revolutionary reconstruction. Naturally, such methods could not fail to lead, with fatal inevitability, into the swamp of conformation, hypocrisy and unprincipledness.

The Brest-Litovsk peace; the agrarian policy with its spasmodic changes from the poorest class of peasantry to the peasant exploiter; the perplexed, panicky attitude to the labour unions; the fitful policy in regard to technical experts, with its theoretical and practical swaying from collegiate management of industries to 'one man power'; nervous appeals to West European capitalism, over the heads of the home and foreign proletariat; finally, the latest inconsistent and zigzaggy, but incontrovertible and assured restoration of the abolished bourgeoisie - such is the new system of Bolshevism. A system of unprecedented shamelessness practiced on a monster scale, a policy of outrageous double-dealing in which the left hand of the Communist Party is beginning consciously to ignore, and even to deny, on principle, what its right hand is doing; when, for instance, it is proclaimed, on the one hand, that the most important problem of the moment is the struggle against the small bourgeoisie (and, incidentally, in stereotyped Bolshevik phraseology, against anarchist elements), while on the other hand are issued new decrees creating the techno-economic and psychological conditions necessary for the restoration and strengthening of that same bourgeoisie - that is the Bolshevik policy that will forever stand as a monument of the thoroughly false, thoroughly contradictory, concerned only in self-preservation, opportunistic policy of the Communist Party dictatorship.

However loud that dictatorship may shout about the great success of its new political methods, it remains the most tragic fact that the worst and most incurable wounds of the Revolution were received at the hands of the Communist dictatorship itself.

An inevitable consequence of Communist Party rule was also the other 'method' of Bolshevik management; terrorism.

Long ago Engels said that the proletariat does not need the State to protect liberty, but needs it for the purpose of crushing its opponents; and that when it will be possible to speak of liberty, there will be no government. The Bolsheviks adopted this maxim not only as their socio-political maxim during the 'transition period', but gave it universal application.

Terrorism always was and still remains the *ultima ratio* of government alarmed for its existence. Terrorism is tempting with its tremendous possibilities. It offers a mechanical solution, as it were, in hopeless situations. Psychologically it is explained as a matter of self defence, as the necessity of throwing off responsibility the better to strike the enemy.

But the principles of terrorism undoubtedly rebound to the fatal injury of liberty and revolution. Absolute power corrupts and defeats its partisans no less than its opponents. A people that knows not liberty becomes accustomed to dictatorship; fighting despotism and counter-revolution, terrorism itself becomes their efficient school.

Once on the road of terrorism, the State necessarily becomes estranged from the people. It must reduce to the possible minimum the circle of persons vested with extraordinary powers, in the name of the safety of the State. And then is born what may be called the panic of authority. The dictator, the despot is always cowardly. He suspects treason everywhere. And the more terrified he becomes, the wilder rages his frightened imagination, incapable of distinguishing real danger from fancied. He sows broadcast discontent, antagonism, hatred Having chosen this course, the State is doomed to follow it to the very end.

The Russian people remained silent, and in their name - in the guise of mortal combat with counter-revolution - the government initiated the most merciless warfare against all political opponents of the Communist Party. Every vestige of liberty was torn out by the roots. Freedom of thought, of the press, of public assembly, self-determination of the worker and of his unions, the freedom of labour - all were declared old rubbish, doctrinaire nonsense, 'bourgeois prejudices', or intrigues of reviving counter-revolution. Science, art, education fell under suspicion. Science is to investigate and teach only the truths of the Communist State; the schools and universities are speedily transformed into Party schools.

Election campaigns, as for instance the recent re-elections to the Moscow Soviet (1921), involve the arrest and imprisonment of opposition candidates who are not favoured by the authorities. With entire impunity the government exposes non-Communist candidates to public insult and derision on the pages of official newspapers pasted on bulletin boards. By numberless stratagems the electors are cajoled and menaced, in turn, and the result of the so-called elections is the complete perversion of the peoples' will.

State terrorism is exercised through government organs known as Extraordinary Commissions. Vested with unlimited powers, independent of any control and practically irresponsible, possessing their own 'simplified' forms of investigation and procedure, with a numerous staff of ignorant, corrupt and brutal agents, these Commissions have within a short time become not only the terror of actual or fancied counter-revolution, but also - and much more so - the most virulent ulcer on the revoltionary body of the country.

The all-pervading secret police methods, the inseparable from them system of provocation, the division of the population into well-meaning and ill-disposed, have gradually transformed the struggle for the new world into an unbridled debauch of espionage, pillage and violence.

No reactionary regime ever dominated the life and liberty of its citizens with such arbitrariness and despotism as the alleged 'dictatorship of the proletariat'. As in the old days of Tsarism, the *okhrana* (secret police section) rules the land. The Soviet prisons are filled with socialists and revolutionists of every shade of political opinion. Physical violence towards political prisoners and hunger strikes in prison are again the order of the day. Summary executions, not only of individuals but *en masse*, are common occurrences. The Socialist State has not scrupled to resort to a measure which even the most brutal bourgeois governments did not dare to use; the system of hostages. Relationship or even casual friendship is sufficient ground for merciless persecution and, quite frequently, for capital punishment.

Gross and barbaric contempt for the most elementary human rights has become an axiom of the Communist Government.

With logical inevitability the Extraordinary Commissions have gradually grown into a monstrous autocratic mechanism, independent and unaccountable, with power over life and death. Appeal is impossible, non-existent. Even the supreme organs of State authority are powerless before the Extraordinary Commissions, as proven by bitter experience.

The Bolshevik Party is not in the habit of scorning any perversion of truth to stigmatise every anti-Bolshevik criticism or protest as 'conspiracy' of one of the 'right' socialist parties; of the social democratic Mensheviks and Socialist Revolutionists. Thus the Communists seek to justify brutal repressions against the 'right elements'. In regard to the Anarchists, however, Bolshevist terrorism cannot be 'justified' by such means.

It is apropos here to sketch, though very briefly, the mutual relations between Anarchism and Bolshevism during the Revolution.

When, in the first days of the Revolution (1917), the labouring masses began the destruction of the system of private ownership and of government, the Anarchists worked shoulder to shoulder with them. The October Revolution instinctively followed the path marked out by the great popular outburst, naturally reflecting Anarchist tendencies. The Revolution destroyed the old State mechanism and pro-

claimed in political life the principle of the federation of soviets. It employed the method of direct expropriation to abolish capitalistic ownership; the peasants and workers expropriated the landlords, chased
the financiers from the banks, seized the factories, mines, mills and
shops. In the field of economic reconstruction the Revolution established the principle of the federation of shop and factory committees
for the management of production. House committees looked after
the assignment of living quarters.

In this early phase of the October Revolution, the Anarchists aided
the people with all the power at their command, and worked hand in
hand with the Bolsheviks in supporting and strengthening the new
principles. Among the legion of enthusiastic fighters of the Revolution, who to the end remained true to the ideals and methods of Anarchism, we may particularly mention here Justin Zhook, the founder
of the famous Schluesselburg powder mill, who lost his life while per-
forming revolutionary military duty; also Zhelesnyakov, who with rare
strength and courage dispersed the Constituent Assembly, and who
afterwards fell fighting against counter-revolutionary invasion.

But as soon as the Bolsheviks succeeded in gaining control of the
movement of the masses, the work of social reconstruction suffered
a sharp change in its character and forms.

From now on the Bolsheviks, under cover of the dictatorship of
the proletariat, use every effort to build up a centralised bureaucratic
State. All who interpreted the Social Revolution as, primarily, the
self-determination of the masses, the introduction of free, non-governmental Communism, - they are henceforth doomed to persecution.
This persecution was directed, first of all, against the critics from 'the
left', the Anarchists. In April, 1918, the ruling Communist Party decided to abolish all Anarchist organisations. Without warning, on the
night of April 12th, the Anarchist club of Moscow was surrounded
by artillery and machine guns, and those present on the premises were
ordered to surrender. Fire was opened on those resisting. The Anarchist quarters were raided, and on the following day the entire Anarchist
press was suppressed.

Since then the persecution of Anarchists and of their organisations
has assumed a systematic character. On the one hand our comrades
were perishing on the military fronts, fighting counter-revolution; on
the other, they were struck down by the Bolshevik State by means
of the Extraordinary Commissions (Cheka).

The further the ruling Party departed from the path marked out by
the October Revolution, the more determinedly it oppressed the other
revolutionary elements and particularly the Anarchists. In November,
1918, the All-Russian Conference of the Anarcho-Syndicalists, held

in Moscow, was arrested *in corpore*. The other Anarchist organisations were broken up and terrorised. Because of the total impossibility of legal activity, some Anarchists decided to 'go underground'. Several of them, in co-operation with some left Socialist Revolutionists, resorted to terrorism. On September 25, 1919, they exploded a bomb in the building (Leontevsky Pereulok) in which the Moscow Committee of the Party was in session. The Anarchist organisations of Moscow, not considering terrorism a solution of the difficulties, publicly expressed disapproval of the tactics of the underground group. The government, however, replied with repressions against **all** Anarchists. Many members of the underground group were executed, a number of Moscow Anarchists were arrested, and in the provinces every expression of the Anarchist movement was suppressed. The finding, during a search, of such Anarchist literature as the works of Kropotkin or Bakunin, led to arrest.

Only in the Ukraina, where the power of the Bolsheviks was comparatively weak, owing to the wide-spread rebel-peasant movement known as the *Makhnovistschina* (from its leader, the Anarchist Makhno), the Anarchist movement continued to some extent active. The advance of Wrangel into the heart of the Ukraina and the inability of the Red Army to halt his progress, caused Makhno temporarily to suspend his struggle with the Bolsheviks for free Soviets and the self determination of the labouring masses. He offered his help to the Bolsheviks to fight the common enemy Wrangel. The offer was accepted, and a contract officially concluded between the Soviet Government and the army of Makhno.

Wrangel was defeated and his army dispersed, with Makhno playing no inconsiderable part in this great military triumph. But with the liquidation of Wrangel, Makhno became unnecessary and dangerous to the Bolsheviks. It was decided to get rid of him, to put an end to *Makhnovistchina*, and, incidentally, dispose of the Anarchists at large. The Bolshevik government betrayed Makhno; the Red forces treacherously surrounded Makhno's army demanding surrender. At the same time all the delegates who had arrived in Kharkov to participate in the Anarchist Congress, for which official permission had been given, were arrested, as well as the Anarchists resident in Kharkov and the comrades still *en route* to the Congress.

Yet, in spite of all the provocative and terroristic tactics of the Bolsheviks against them, the Anarchists of Russia refrained, during the whole period of civil war, from protesting to the workers of Europe and America - aye, even to those of Russia itself - fearing that such action might be prejudicial to the interests of the Russian Revolution and that it may aid the common enemy, world imperialism.

But with the termination of civil war the position of the Anarchists grew even worse. The new policy of the Bolsheviks of open compromise with the bourgeois world became clearer, more definite, and ever sharper their break with the revolutionary aspirations of the working masses. The struggle against Anarchism, till then often masked by the excuse of fighting 'banditism in the guise of Anarchism', now became open and frank warfare against Anarchist ideals and ideas, as such.

The Kronstadt events offered the Bolsheviks the desired pretext for completely 'liquidating' the Anarchists. Wholesale arrests were instituted throughout Russia. Irrespective of factional adherence, practically all known Russian Anarchists were taken into the police net. To this day all of them remain in prison, without any charges having been preferred against them. In the night of April 25th-26th, 1921, all the political prisoners in the Bootirka prison (Moscow), to the number of over 400, consisting of representatives of the right and left wings of socialist parties and members of Anarchist organisations, were forcibly taken from the prison and transferred. On that occasion many of the prisoners suffered brutal violence; women were dragged down the steps by their hair, and a number of the politicals sustained serious injuries. The prisoners were divided into several groups and sent to various prisons in the provinces. Of their further fate we have so far been unable to receive definite information.*

Thus did the Bolsheviks reply to the revolutionary enthusiasm and deep faith which inspired the masses in the beginning of their great struggle for liberty and justice - a reply that expressed itself in the policy of compromise abroad and terrorism at home.

This policy proved fatal; it corrupted and disintegrated the Revolution, poisoned it, slayed its soul, destroyed its moral, spiritual significance. By its despotism; by stubborn, petty paternalism; by the perfidy which replaced its former revolutionary idealism; by its stifling formalism and criminal indifference to the interests and aspirations of the masses; by its cowardly suspicion and distrust of the people at large, the 'dictatorship of the proletariat' hopelessly cut itself off from the labouring masses.

Thrust back from direct participation in the constructive work of the Revolution, harassed at every step, the victim of constant super-

*This pamphlet was written in June 1921. Since then some of the anarchists imprisoned in Moscow have been deported from Russia, though natives of that country; others have been exiled to distant parts, while a large number are still in the prisons. (A.B.)

vision and control by the Party, the proletariat is becoming accustomed to consider the Revolution and its further fortunes as the private, personal affair of the Bolsheviks. In vain does the Communist Party seek by ever new decrees to preserve its hold upon the country's life. The people have seen through the real meaning of the Party dictatorship. They know its narrow, selfish dogmatism, its cowardly opportunism; they are aware of its internal decay, its intrigues behind the scenes.

In the land where, after three years of tremendous effort, of terrible and heroic sacrifice, there should have come to bloom the wonder-flower of Communism, - alas, even its withered buds are killed in distrust, apathy, and enmity.

Thus came about the era of revolutionary stagnation, of sterility, which cannot be cured by any political party methods, and which demonstrates the complete social atrophy.

The swamp of compromise into which Bolshevik dictatorship had sunk proved fatal to the Revolution; it became poisoned by its noxious miasma. In vain do the Bolsheviks point to the imperialistic world as the cause of Russia's economic breakdown; in vain do they ascribe it to the blockade and the attacks of armed counter-revolution. Not in them is the real source of the collapse and debacle.

No blockade, no wars with foreign reaction could dismay or conquer the revolutionary people whose unexampled heroism, self-sacrifice and perseverance defeated all its external enemies. On the contrary, it is probable that civil war really helped the Bolsheviks. It served to keep alive popular enthusiasm and nurtured the hope that, with the end of the war, the ruling Communist Party will make effective the new revolutionary principles and secure the people in the enjoyment of the fruits of the Revolution. The masses looked forward to the yearned-for opportunity for social and economic liberty. Paradoxical as it may sound, the Communist dictatorship had no better ally, in the sense of strengthening and prolonging its life, than the reactionary forces which fought against it.

It was only the termination of the wars which permitted a full view of the economic and psychologic demoralisation to which the blindly despotic policy of the dictatorship brought the revolutionary country. Then it became evident that the most formidable danger to the Revolution was not outside, but **within** the country; a danger resulting from the very nature of the social and economic arrangements which characterise the present 'transitory stage'.

We fully realise the gross error of the theoreticians of bourgeois political economy who wilfully ignore the study of industrial evolution from the historico-social viewpoint, and stupidly confound the system of State capitalism with that of the socialist dictatorship. The Bolsheviks are quite right when they insist that the two types of soc-io-economic development are 'diametrically opposed in their essential character'. However, it were wrong and useless to pretend that such a form of industrial life as expressed in the present system of prolet-arian dictatorship is anything essentially different from State capital-ism.

As a matter of fact, the proletarian dictatorship, as it actually ex-ists, is in no sense different from State capitalism.

The distinctive characteristics of the latter - inherent social antag-onisms - are abolished only formally in the Soviet Republic. In real-ity those antagonisms exist and are very deep-seated. The exploitat-ion of labour, the enslavement of the worker and peasant, the cancel-lation of the citizen as a human being, as a personality, and his trans-formation into a microscopic part of the universal economic mechan-ism owned by the government; the system of compulsory labour serv-ice and its punitive organs - such are the characteristic features of State capitalism.

All these features are also to be found in the present Russian sys-tem. It were unpardonable naivity, or still more unpardonable hypoc-risy, to pretend - as do Bolshevik theoreticians, especially Bukharin - that universal compulsory labour service in the system of the prolet-arian dictatorship is, in contradistinction to State capitalism, 'the self-organisation of the masses for purposes of labour', or that the existing 'mobilisation of industry is the strengthening of socialism', and that 'State coercion in the system of proletarian dictatorship is a means of building the Communist society'.

A year ago Trotsky, at the 10th Congress of the Communist Party of Russia, thundered against the 'bourgeois notion' that compulsory labour is not productive. He sought to convince his audience that the main problem is to 'draw the worker into the process of labour, not by external methods of coercion, but by means internal, psycholog-ical'. But when he approached the concrete application of this princ-iple, he advocated a 'very complex system, involving methods of an ethical nature, as well as premiums and **punishment**, in order to in-crease the productivity of labour in consonance with those principles of compulsion according to which we are constructing our whole ec-onomic life'.

The experiment was made, and it gave surprising results. Whether the old 'bourgeois notion' proved correct, or the newest socialism was powerless 'internally, psychologically compulsory' to 'draw the worker into the process of production', by means of premiums, pun-ishment, etc., at any rate, the worker refused to be snared by the tempting formula of 'psychologic coercion'. Evidently the ideology as well as the practice of Bolshevism convinced the toilers that the socio-economic ideals of the Bolsheviks are incidentally also a step forward in the more intensive exploitation of labour. For Bolshevism, far from saving the country from ruin and in no way improving the conditions of existence for the masses, is attempting to turn the serf of yesterday into a complete slave. How little the Communist State is concerned about the workers' well-being is seen from the statement of a prominent Communist delegate to the 10th Congress of the Party; 'Up till now Soviet policy has been characterised by the complete absence of any plan to improve the living conditions of labour'. And further; 'All that was done in that regard happened accidentally, or was done by fits and starts, by local authorities under pressure of the masses themselves'.

Is this, then, the system of proletarian dictatorship or State capitalism?

Chained to their work, deprived of the right to leave the job on pain of prison or summary execution for 'labour desertion'; bossed and spied upon by Party overseers; divided into qualified sheep (artisans) and unqualified goats (labourers) receiving unequal food rations; hungry and insufficiently clad, deprived of the right to protest or strike - such are the modern proletarians of the Communist dictatorship. Is this 'self-organisation' of the toiling masses not a step backward, a return to feudal serfdom or negro slavery? Is the hand of the Communist State executioner less ruthless than the whip of the plantation boss? Only scholasticism or blind fanaticism can see in this, the most grievous form of slavery, the emancipation of labour or even the least approach to it.

It is the height of tragedy that State Socialism, enmeshed in logical antitheses, could give to the world nothing better than the intensification of the evils of the very system whose antagonisms produced socialism.

The Party dictatorship applies the same policy, in every detail, also to the peasantry. Here, too, the State is the universal master. The same policy of compulsory labour, of oppression, spying, and systematic expropriation of the fruits of the peasant's toil; the former method of requisition which frequently stripped the peasants even of the necessaries of life; or the newly initiated, but no less predatory, food tax; the senseless, enormous waste of foodstuffs due to the cumbrous system of centralisation and the Bolshevik food policy; the dooming of whole peasant districts to slow starvation, disease and death; punitive expeditions, massacring peasant families by the wholesale and razing entire villages to the ground for the slightest resistance to the plundering policy of the Communist dictatorship - such are the methods of Bolshevik rule.

Thus, neither economic nor political exploitation of the industrial and agrarian proletariat has ceased. Only its forms have changed; formerly exploitation was purely capitalistic; now, labeled 'workers' and peasants' government' and christened 'communist economy', it is State capitalistic.

But this modern system of State capitalism is pernicious not only because it degrades the living human into a soulless machine. It contains another, no less destructive, element. By its very nature this system is extremely aggressive. Far from abolishing militarism, in the narrow sense of the term, it applies the principle of militarisation - with all its attributes of mechanical discipline, irresponsible authority and repression - to every phase of human effort.

Socialist militarisation is not only admitted, but defended and justified by the theoreticians of the Party. Thus Bukharin in his work on the 'Economics of the Transition Period' writes; 'The workers' government, when waging war, seeks to broaden and strengthen the economic foundations on which it is built - that is, socialist forms of production. Incidentally, it is clear from this that, in principle, even an aggressive revolutionary socialist war is permissible'. And, indeed, we are already familiar with some imperialistic pretensions of the 'workers' dictatorship.

Thus the 'bourgeois prejudices' kicked out through the window re-enter through the door.

It is evident that the militarism of the 'labour' dictatorship, like any other militarism, necessitates the formation of a gigantic army of non-producers. Moreover, such an army and all its various organs must be supplied with technical resources and means of existence, which puts additional burdens on the producers, that is, the workers and the peasants.

Another and the most momentous internal danger is the dictatorship itself. The dictatorship which, despotic and ruthless, has alienated itself from the labouring masses, has strangled initiative and liberty, supressed the creative spirit of the very elements which bore the brunt of the Revolution, and is slowly but effectively instilling its poison in the hearts and minds of Russia.

Thus does the dictatorship itself sow counter-revolution. Not conspiracies from without, not the campaigns of the Denikins and Wrangels are the Damocles sword of Russia. The real and greatest danger is that country-wide dissillusionment, resentment and hatred of Bolshevik despotism, that counter- revolutionary attitude of the people at large, which is the legitimate offspring of the Communist Party dictatorship itself.

Even in the ranks of the proletariat is ripening, with cumulative force, the protest against the reactionary 'big stick' policy of Bolshevism.

The organised labour movement of Russia developed immediately after the February Revolution. The formation of shop and factory committees was the first step toward actual control by labour of the activities of the capitalist owners. Such control, however, could not be general without co-ordinating the work of all other similar committees, and thus came to life Soviets, or General Councils, of shop and factory committees, and their All-Russian Congress.

In this manner the shop and factory committees (*zahvkomy*) were the pioneers in labour control of industry, with the prospect of themselves, in the near future, managing the industries entire. The labour unions, on the other hand, were engaged in improving the living conditions and cultural environment of their membership.

But after the October Revolution the situation changed. The centralisation methods of the Bolshevik dictatorship penetrated also into the unions. The autonomy of the shop committees was now declared superfluous. The labour unions were reorganised on industrial principles, with the shop committee emasculated into a mere 'embryo' of the union, and entirely subjected to the authority of the central organs. Thus all independence of action, all initiative was torn from the hands of the workers themselves and transferred to the union bureaucracy. The result of this policy was the complete indifference of the workers to their unions and to the fate of the industries.

Then the Communist Party began to fill the labour unions with its own party members. **They occupied the union offices.** That was easily done because all the other political parties were outlawed and there existed no public press except the official Bolshevik publications. No wonder that within a short time the Communists proved an overwhelming majority in all the provincial and central executive committees, and had in their hands the exclusive management of the labour unions. They usurped the dominant role in every labour body, including even such organisations where the membership (as in the Union of Soviet Employees) is manifestly and most bitterly opposed to the Bolsheviks. Whenever an occasional union proved refractory, as the printers, for instance, and refused to yield to 'internal psychologic persuasion', the Communists solved the difficulty by the simple expedient of suspending the entire administration of the union.

Having gained control of the political machinery of the labour organisations, the Communist Party formed in every shop and factory small groups of its own members, so-called Communist 'cells', which became the practical masters of the situation. The Communist 'cell' is vested with such powers that no action of the shop or factory committee (even if the latter consist of Communists) is valid unless sanctioned by the 'cell'. The highest organ of the labour movement, the All-Russian Central Soviet of Labour Unions, is itself under the direct control of the Central Committee of the Communist Party.

Lenin and other Bolshevik leaders take the position that the labour union must be, first and foremost, a 'school of Communism'. In practice the role of the labour union in Russia is reduced to that of an automatic agency for the execution of the orders of the ruling Party.

However, this state of affairs is becoming unbearable even to that labour element which is still faithful to the commandments of State Communism. In the ranks of the Communist Party itself there has developed an opposition movement against the military governmentalisation of the labour unions. This new movement, known as the Workers' Opposition, though still loyal to its Communist parent, yet realises the full horror of the hopeless position, the 'blind alley' into which the criminally stupid policies of the Bolsheviks have driven the Russian proletariat and the Revolution.

The Workers' Opposition is characterised by the good orthodox Communist Kolontai as 'the advance guard of the proletariat, class conscious and welded by the ties of class interests', an element which 'has not estranged itself from the rank and file of the working masses and has not become lost among Soviet office holders'. This Workers' Opposition protests 'against the bureaucratisation, against the differentiation between the "upper" and the "lower" people', against the excesses of the Party hegemony, and against the shifting and twisting policy of the ruling central power. 'The great creative and constructive power of the proletariat', says the Workers' Opposition, 'cannot be replaced, in the task of building the Communist society, by the mere emblem of the dictatorship of the working class', - of that dictatorship which a prominent Communist characterised at the last Congress of the Communist Party as 'the dictatorship of the Party bureacracy'.

Indeed, the Workers' Opposition is justified in asking, 'Are we, the proletariat, really the backbone of the working class dictatorship, or are we to be considered as a will-less herd, good enough to carry on our backs some party politicians who are pretending to reconstruct the economic life of the country without our control, without our constructive class spirit?'

And this Workers' Opposition, according to Kolontai, 'keeps on growing in spite of the determined resistance on the part of the most influential leaders of the Party, and gains more and more adherents among the labouring masses throughout Russia'.

But the 10th Congress of the Communist Party of Russia (April, 1921) put its decisive veto on the Workers' Opposition. Henceforth it is officially doomed, discussion of its ideas and principles forbidden because of 'their Anarcho-syndicalist tendency', as Lenin expressed himself. The Communist Party declared war on the Workers' Opposition. The Party Congress decided that 'propagation of the principles of the Labour Opposition is incompatible with membership in the Communist Party'. The demand to turn the management of the industries over to the proletariat was outlawed.

The October Revolution was initiated with the great battle cry of the First International, 'The emancipation of the workers must be accomplished by the workers themselves'. Yet we saw that, when the period of constructive destruction had passed, when the foundations of Tsarism had been razed, and the bourgeois system abolished, the Communist Party thought itself sufficiently strong to take into its own hands the entire management of the country. It began the education of the workers in a spirit of strictest authoritarianism, and step by step the Soviet system became transformed into a bureaucratic, punitive police machine. Terrorism became its logical, inevitable handmaid.

General indifference and hatred, and complete social paralysis, were the result of the government course. An atmosphere of slavish submission, at once revolting and disgusting, pervades the whole country. It stifles alike the oppressed and the oppressors.

What boots it that the sober minded, compromise ready Lenin begins his every speech with the confession of the many and serious mistakes which have been made by the Party in power? No piling up of mistakes by the 'ingenious opportunist', as Lunacharsky dubs Lenin, can dismay the champions of Bolshevism intoxicated with their Party's political dominion. The mistakes of their leaders become, in the interpretation of Communist theoreticians and publicists, 'eminent necessity', and the convulsive attempts to correct them (the whole agrarian policy) are hailed as acts of the greatest wisdom, humanity and loyalty to Bolshevik principles.

In vain the impatient cry of Kolontai; 'The fear of criticism, inherent in our system of bureaucracy, at times reaches the point of caricature'. The Party Elders brand her a heretic for her pains, her pamphlet 'The Workers' Opposition' is prohibited and Illych himself (Lenin) 'settles' her with a few sarcastic personal slurs. The syndicalist 'peril' is supposedly removed.

Meanwhile the Opposition is growing, deepening, spreading throughout working Russia.

Indeed, what shall the impartial observer think of the peculiar picture presented by Bolshevik Russia? Numerous labour strikes, with scores of workers arrested and often summarily executed; peasant uprisings and revolts, continuous revolutionary insurrections in various parts of the country. Is it not a terribly tragic situation, a heinous absurdity? Is not the rebellion of workers and peasants, however lacking in class consciousness in some cases, actual war against the workers' and peasants' government - the very government which is flesh of the flesh and blood of the blood of themselves, which had been called to guard their interests, and whose existence should be possible only in so far as it corresponds to the needs and demands of the labouring masses?

The popular protests do not cease. The opposition movement grows, and in self-defence the Party must, from time to time, mollify the people, even at the sacrifice of its principles. But where it is impossible by a few sops to still the craving for bread and liberty, the hungry mouths are shut with bullet or bayonet, and the official press brands the protestants with the infamous name of 'counter-revolutionists', traitors against the 'workers' and peasants' government'.

Then Russia, Bolshevik Russia, is quiet again - with the quietness of death.

The history of recent days is filled with gruesome illustrations of such quiet.

One of those illustrations is Kronstadt - Kronstadt, against which has been perpetrated the most awful crime of the Party dictatorship, a crime against the proletariat, against socialism, against the Revolution. A crime multiplied a hundredfold by the deliberate and perfidious lies spread by the Bolsheviks throughout the world.

Future history will deal adequately with this crying shame. Here we shall give but a brief sketch of the Kronstadt events.

In the month of February, 1921, the workers of four Petrograd factories went on strike. It had been an exceptionally hard winter for them; they and their families suffered from cold, hunger and exhaustion. They demanded an increase of their food rations, some fuel and clothing. Here and there was also voiced the demand for the Constituent Assembly and free trade. The strikers attempted a street demonstration, and the authorities ordered out the military against them, chiefly the *kursanti*, the young Communists of the military training schools.

When the Kronstadt sailors learned what was happening in Petrograd, they expressed their solidarity with the strikers in their economic and revolutionary demands, but refused to support any call for the Constituent Assembly and free trade. On March 1, the sailors organised a mass-meeting in Kronstadt which was attended also by the Chairman of the All-Russian Central Executive Committee, Kalinin, (the presiding officer of the Republic of Russia), by the Commander of the Fortress of Kronstadt, Kuzmin, and by the Chairman of the Kronstadt Soviet, Vassilyev. The meeting, held with the knowledge and permission of the Executive Committee of the Kronstadt Soviet, passed resolutions approved by the sailors, the garrison and the citizen meeting of 16,000 persons. Kalinin, Kuzmin and Vassilyev spoke against the resolutions. The main points of the latter were; free speech and free press for the revolutionary parties; amnesty for imprisoned revolutionists; re-election of the Soviets by secret ballot and freedom from government interference during the electioneering campaign.

The Bolshevik authorities replied to the resolutions by beginning to remove from the city the food and ammunition supplies. The sailors prevented the attempt, closed the entrances to the city, and arrested some of the more obstreperous commissars. Kalinin was permitted to return to Petrograd.

No sooner did the Petrograd authorities learn of the Kronstadt resolutions, than they initiated a campaign of lies and libel. In spite of the fact that Zinoviev kept in constant telephonic communication with the presiding officer of the Kronstadt Soviet, and was assured by the latter that all was quiet in Kronstadt and that the sailors were busy only with preparations for the re-elections, the Petrograd radio station was kept hard at work sending messages to the world announcing a counter-revolutionary conspiracy and a white-guard uprising in Kronstadt. At the same time Zinoviev, Kalinin and their aides succeeded in persuading the Petrograd Soviet to pass a resolution which was an ultimatum to Kronstadt to surrender immediately, on pain of complete annihilation in case of refusal.

A group of well-known and trusted revolutionists, then in Petrograd, realising the provocative character of such a policy, appealed to Zinoviev and to the Council of Defence, of which he was the President. They pointed out the unrevolutionary, reactionary nature of his policy and its great danger to the Revolution. The demands of Kronstadt were clearly set forth; they were against the Constituent Assembly, against free trade, and in favour of the Soviet form of government. But the people of Kronstadt, as they frankly stated in their bulletin, could no longer tolerate the despotism of the Party, and demanded the right to air their grievances and the re-establishment of free Soviets. 'All power to the Soviets' was again their watchword, as it had been that of the people and of the Bolsheviks in 1917. To resort to armed force against Kronstadt were the height of folly; indeed a terrible crime. The only right and revolutionary solution lay in complying with the request of Kronstadt (wired by the sailors to Zinoviev, but not transmitted by him to the Soviet) for the selection of an impartial Commission to reach an amicable settlement.

But this appeal of the Petrograd group of revolutionaries was ignored. Many Communists clearly understood how maliciously reactionary was the government attitude toward Kronstadt, but slavishly debased and morally crippled by the jesuitism of the Party, they dared not speak and mutely participated in the crime.

On March 7th Trotsky began the bombardment of Kronstadt, and on the 17th the fortress and city were taken, after numerous fierce assaults involving terrific human sacrifice and treachery. Thus Kronstadt was 'liquidated', and the 'counter-revolutionary plot' quenched in blood. The 'conquest' of the city was characterised by ruthless savagery to the defeated, although not a single one of the Communists arrested by the Kronstadt sailors had been injured or killed by them. And even before the storming of the fortress the Bolsheviks summarily executed numerous soldiers of the Red Army, whose revolutionary spirit and solidarity caused them to refuse to participate in the blood bath.

The 'conspiracy' and the 'victory' were necessary for the Communist Party to save it from threatening inner decomposition. Trotsky, who during the discussion of the role of the Labour Unions (at the joint session of the Communist Party, the Central Executive Council of the Unions, and the delegates to the 6th Congress of the Soviets, December 30th, 1920) was treated as a bad boy who 'don't know his Marx', once more proved himself the saviour of the 'country in danger'. Harmony was re-established.

A few days after the 'glorious conquest' of Kronstadt, Lenin said at the 10th Congress of the Communist Party of Russia; 'The sailors did not want the counter-revolutionists, but - they did not want us either'. And, - irony of the executioner! - at that very Congress Lenin advocated **free trade**, 'as a respite'.

On March 17th the Communist government celebrated its bloody victory over the Kronstadt proletariat, and on the 18th it commemorated the martyrs of the Paris Commune. As if it was not evident to all who had eyes and would see, that the crime committed at Kronstadt was far more terrible and enormous than the slaughter of the Commune in 1871, for it was done in the name of the Social Revolution, in the name of the Socialist Republic. Henceforth to the vile classic figures of Thiers and Gallifet are added those of Trotsky, Zinoviev, Dihbenko, Tukhachefsky.

Thus is human sacrifice brought to the Moloch of Bolshevism, to the gigantic lie that is still growing and spreading throughout the world and enmeshing it in its network of ruin, falsehood and treachery. Nor is it only the liberty and lives of individual citizens which are sacrificed to this god of clay, nor even merely the well-being of the country; it is socialist ideals and the fate of the Revolution which are being destroyed.

Long ago Bakunin wrote; 'The whole power of the Russian Tsar is built upon a lie - a lie at home and a lie abroad; a colossal and artful system of lies never witnessed before, perhaps, in the whole history of man'.

But now such a system exists. It is the system of State Communism. The revolutionary proletariat of the world must open their eyes to the real situation in Russia. They should learn to see what a terrible abyss the ruling Bolshevik Party, by its blind and bloody dictatorship, has brought Russia and the Russian Revolution. Let the world proletariat give ear to the voices of true revolutionists, the voices of those whose object is not political party power, but the success of the Social Revolution, and to whom the Revolution is synonymous with human dignity, liberty and social regeneration.

May the proletariat of Europe and America, when the world revolution comes, choose a different road than the one followed by the Bolsheviks. The road of Bolshevism leads to the formation of a social regime with new class antagonisms and class distinctions; it leads to State capitalism, which only the blind fanatic can consider as a transition stage toward a free society in which all class differences are abolished.

State Communism, the contemporary Soviet government, is not and can never become the threshold of a free, voluntary, non-authoritarian Communist society, because the very essence and nature of governmental, compulsory Communism excludes such an evolution. Its consistent economic and political centralisation, its governmentalism and bureaucratisation of every sphere of human activity and effort, its inevitable militarisation and degradation of the human spirit mechanically destroy every germ of new life and extinguish the stimuli of creative, constructive work.

It is the Communist Party dictatorship **itself** which most effectively hinders the further development and deepening of the Revolution.

The historic struggle of the labouring masses for liberty necessarily and unavoidably proceeds outside the sphere of governmental influence. The struggle against oppression - political, economic and social - against the exploitation of man by man, or of the individual by the government, is always simultaneously also a struggle against government as such. The political State, whatever its form, and constructive revolutionary effort are irreconcilable. They are mutually exclusive. Every revolution in the course of its development faces this alternative; to build freely, independent and despite of the government, or to choose government with all the limitation and stagnation it involves. The path of the Social Revolution, of the constructive self-reliance of the organised, conscious masses, is in the direction of non-government, that is, of Anarchy. Not the State, not government, but systematic and co-ordinated social reconstruction by the toilers is necessary for the upbuilding of the new, free society. Not the State and its police methods, but the solidaric co-operation of all working elements - the proletariat, the peasantry, the revolutionary intelligentsia - mutually helping each other in their voluntary associations, will emancipate us from the State superstition and bridge the passage between the abolished old civilisation and Free Communism. Not by order of some central authority, but organically, from life itself, must grow up the closely-knit federation of the united industrial, agrarian, etc. associations; by the workers themselves must it be organised and managed, and then - and only then - will the great aspiration of labour for social regeneration have a sound, firm foundation. Only such an organisation of the commonwealth will make room for the really free, creative, new humanity, and will be the actual threshold of non-governmental, Anarchist Communism.

Thus, and only thus, can be completely swept away all the remnants of our old, dying civilisation, and the human mind and heart relieved of the varied poisons of ignorance and prejudice.

The revolutionary world proletariat must be permitted to hear this Anarchist voice, which cries to them - as of yore - from the depths, from the prison dungeons.

The world proletariat should understand the great tragedy of the toilers of Russia; the heart-breaking tragedy of the workers and peasants who bore the brunt of the Revolution and who find themselves now helpless in the iron clutch of an all-paralysing State. The world proletariat must, ere too late, loosen that stranglehold.

If not, then Soviet Russia, once the hearth of the Social Revolution of the world, will again become the world's haven of blackest reaction.

The Kronstadt Rebellion

1   Labour Disturbances in Petrograd

It was early in 1921. Long years of war, revolution, and civil struggle had bled Russia to exhaustion and brought her people to the brink of despair. But at last civil war was at an end; the numerous fronts were liquidated, and Wrangel - the last hope of Entente intervention and Russian counter-revolution - was defeated and his military activities within Russia terminated. The people now confidently looked forward to the mitigation of the severe Bolshevik regime. It was expected that with the end of civil war the Communists would lighten the burdens, abolish war-time restrictions, introduce some fundamental liberties, and begin the organisation of a more normal life. Though far from being popular, the Bolshevik government had the support of the workers in its oft announced plan of taking up the economic reconstruction of the country as soon as military operations should cease. The people were eager to co-operate, to put their initiative and creative efforts to the upbuilding of the ruined land.

Most unfortunately, these expectations were doomed to disappointmant. The Communist State showed no intention of loosening the yoke. The same policies continued, with labour militarisation still further enslaving the people, embittering them with added oppression and tyranny, and in consequence paralysing every possibility of industrial revival. The last hope of the proletariat was perishing; the conviction grew that the Communist Party was more interested in retaining political power than in saving the Revolution.

The most revolutionary elements of Russia, the workers of Petrograd, were the first to speak out. They charged that, aside from other causes, Bolshevik centralisation, bureaucracy, and autocratic attitude toward the peasants and workers were directly responsible for much of the misery and suffering of the people. Many factories and mills of Petrograd had been closed, and the workers were literally starving. They called meetings to consider the situation. The meetings were suppressed by the government. The Petrograd proletariat, who had borne the brunt of the revolutionary struggles and whose great sacrifices and heroism alone had saved the city from Yudenitch, resented the action of the government. Feeling against the methods employed by the Bolsheviks continued to grow. More meetings were called with the same result. The Communists would make no concessions to the proletariat, while at the same time they were offering to compromise with the capitalists of Europe and America. The workers were indignant - they became aroused. To compel the government to listen to their demands, strikes were called in the Patronny munition works, the Trubotchny and Baltiyski mills, and in the Laferm factory. Instead of talking matters over with the dissatisfied workers, the 'Workers' and Peasants' Government' created a war-time *Komitet Oborony* (Committee of Defence) with Zinoviev, the most hated man in Petrograd, as Chairman. The avowed purpose of that Committee was to suppress the strike movement.

It was on February 24th that the strikes were declared. The same day the Bolsheviks sent the *kursanti*, the Communist students of the military academy (training officers for the Army and Navy), to disperse the workers who had gathered on Vassilevsky Ostrov, the labour district of Petrograd. The next day, February 25th, the indignant strikers of Vassilevsky Ostrov visited the Admiralty shops and the Galernaya docks, and induced the workers there to join their protest against the autocratic attitude of the Government. The attempted street demonstration of the strikers was dispersed by armed soldiery.

On February 26th the Petrograd Soviet held a session at which the prominent Communist Lashevitch, member of the Committee of Defence and of the Revolutionary Military Soviet of the Republic, denounced the strike movement in sharpest terms. He charged the workers of the Trubotchny factory with inciting dissatisfaction, accused them of being 'self-seeking labour skinners (*shkurniki*) and counter-revolutionists', and proposed that the Trubotchny factory be closed. The Executive Committee of the Petrograd Soviet (Zinoviev, Chairman) accepted the suggestion. The Trubotchny strikers were **locked out** and thus automatically deprived of their rations.

These methods of the Bolshevik Government served still further to embitter and antagonise the workers.

Strikers' proclamations now began to appear on the streets of Petrograd. Some of them assumed a distinctly political character, the most significant of them, posted on the walls of the city February 27, reading;

A complete change is necessary in the policies of the Government. First of all, the workers and peasants need freedom. They don't want to live by the decrees of the Bolsheviks; they want to control their own destinies.

Comrades, preserve revolutionary order! Determinedly and in an organised manner demand -

Liberation of all arrested socialists and non-partisan working-men.

Abolition of martial law; freedom of speech, press and assembly for all who labour.

Free election of shop and factory committees (*zahvkomi*), of labour, union and soviet representatives.

Call meetings, pass resolutions, send your delegates to the authorities and work for the realisation of your demands.

The government replied to the demands of the strikers by making numerous arrests and suppressing several labour organisations. The action resulted in popular temper growing more anti-Bolshevik; reactionary slogans began to be heard. Thus on February 28 there appeared a proclamation of the 'Socialist Workers of the Nevsky District', which concluded with a call for the Constituent Assembly;

We know who is afraid of the Constituent Assembly. It is they who will no longer be able to rob the people. Instead they will have to answer before the representatives of the people for their deceit, their robberies, and all their crimes.

Down with the hated Communists!

Down with the Soviet Government!

Long live the Constituent Assembly!

Meanwhile the Bolsheviks concentrated in Petrograd large military forces from the provinces and also ordered to the city its most trusted Communist regiments from the front. Petrograd was put under 'extraordinary martial law'. The strikers were overawed, and the labour unrest crushed with an iron hand.

2   The Kronstadt Movement

The Kronstadt sailors were much disturbed by what was happening in Petrograd. They did not look with friendly eyes upon the government's drastic treatment of the strikers. They knew what the revolutionary proletariat of the capital had had to bear since the first days of the Revolution, how heroically they had fought against Yudenitch, and how patiently they were suffering privation and misery. But Kronstadt was far from favouring the Constitutional Assembly or the demand for free trade which made itself heard in Petrograd. The sailors were thoroughly revolutionary in spirit and action. They were the staunchest supporters of the Soviet system, but they were opposed to the dictatorship of any political party.

The sympathetic movement with the Petrograd strikers first began among the sailors of the warships *Petropavlovsk* and *Sevastopol* - the ships that in 1917 had been the main support of the Bolsheviks. The movement spread to the whole fleet of Kronstadt, then to the Red Army regiments stationed there. On February 28 the men of *Petropavlosk* passed a resolution which was also concurred in by the sailors of *Sevastopol*. The resolution demanded, among other things, free re-elections to the Kronstadt Soviet, as the tenure of office of the latter was about to expire. At the same time a committee of sailors was sent to Petrograd to learn the situation there.

On March 1 a public meeting was held on the Yakorny Square in Kronstadt, which was officially called by the crews of the First and Second Squadrons of the Baltic Fleet. 16,000 sailors, Red Army men, and workers attended the gathering. It was presided over by the Chairman of the Executive Committee of the Kronstadt Soviet, the Communist Vassiliev. The President of the Russian Socialist Federated Republic, Kalinin, and the Commissar of the Baltic Fleet, Kuzmin, were present and addressed the audience. It may be mentioned, as indicative of the friendly attitude of the sailors to the Bolshevik government, that Kalinin was met on his arrival in Kronstadt with military honours, music, and banners.

At this meeting the Sailors' Committee that had been sent to Petrograd on February 28 made its report. It corroborated the worst fears of Kronstadt. The audience was outspoken in its indignation at the methods used by the Communists to crush the modest demands of the Petrograd workers. The resolution which had been passed by *Petropavlovsk* on February 28 was then submitted to the meeting. President Kalinin and Commissar Kuzmin bitterly attacked the resolution and denounced the Petrograd strikers as well as the Kronstadt sailors. But their arguments failed to impress the audience, and the *Petropavlovsk* resolution was passed unanimously. The historic document read -

Resolution of the General Meeting of the Crews of the First and Second Squadrons of the Baltic Fleet, held March 1, 1921

Having heard the Report of the Representatives sent by the

General Meeting of Ship Crews to Petrograd to investigate the situation there, Resolved;

1) In view of the fact that the present Soviets do not express the will of the workers and peasants, immediately to hold new elections by secret ballot, the pre-election campaign to have full freedom of agitation among the workers and peasants;

2) To establish freedom of speech and press for workers and peasants, for Anarchists and left Socialist parties;

3) To secure freedom of assembly for labour unions and peasant organisations;

4) To call a non-partisan Conference of the workers, Red Army soldiers and sailors of Petrograd, Kronstadt, and of Petrograd Province, no later than March 10, 1921;

5) To liberate all political prisoners of Socialist parties, as well as all workers, peasants, soldiers, and sailors imprisoned in connection with the labour and peasant movements;

6) To elect a Commission to review the cases of those held in prisons and concentration camps;

7) To abolish all *politodeli* (political bureaus) because no party should be given special privileges in the propagation of its ideas or receive the financial support of the Government for such purposes. Instead there should be established educational and cultural commissions, locally elected and financed by the Government;

8) To abolish immediately all *zagryaditelniye otryadi*;*

9) To equalise the rations of all who work, with the exception of those employed in trades detrimental to health;

10) To abolish the Communist fighting detachments in all branches of the Army, as well as the Communist guards kept on duty in mills and factories. Should such guards of military detachments be found necessary, they are to be appointed in the Army from the ranks, and in the factories according to the judgement of the workers;

11) To give the peasants full freedom of action in regard to their land, and also the right to keep cattle, on condition that the peasants manage with their own means, that is, without employing hired labour;

12) To request all branches of the Army, as well as our comrades the military *kursanti*, to concur in our resolutions;

13) To demand that the press give the fullest publicity to our resolutions;

*Armed units organised by the Bolsheviks for the purpose of suppressing traffic and confiscating foodstuffs and other products. The irresponsibility and arbitrariness of their methods were proverbial throughout the country. The Government abolished them in the Petrograd Province on the eve of its attack against Kronstadt - a bribe to the Petrograd proletariat. (A.B.)

RT-E

14) To appoint a Travelling Commission of Control;

15) To permit free *kustarnoye* (individual small scale) production by one's own efforts.

Resolution passed unanimously by Brigade Meeting, two persons refraining from voting.

Petrichenko
Chairman Brigade Meeting
Perepelkin
Secretary

Resolution passed by an overwhelming majority of the Kronstadt garrison.

Vassiliev
Chairman

Together with comrade Kalinin Vassiliev votes against the resolution.

This Resolution, strenuously opposed - as already mentioned - by Kalinin and Kuzmin, was passed over their protest. After the meeting Kalinin was permitted to return to Petrograd unmolested.

At the same Brigade Meeting it was also decided to send a Committee to Petrograd to explain to the workers and the garrison there the demands of Kronstadt and to request that non-partisan delegates be sent by the Petrograd proletariat to Kronstadt to learn the actual state of affairs and the demands of the sailors. This Committee, which consisted of thirty members, was arrested by the Bolsheviks in Petrograd. It was the first blow struck by the Communist Government against Kronstadt. The fate of the Committee remained a mystery.

As the term of office of the members of the Kronstadt Soviet was about to expire, the Brigade Meeting also decided to call a Conference of delegates on March 2, to discuss the manner in which the new elections were to be held. The Conference was to consist of representatives of the ships, the garrison, the various Soviet institutions, the labour unions and factories, each organisation to be represented by two delegates.

The Conference of March 2 took place in the House of Education (the former Kronstadt School of Engineering) and was attended by over 300 delegates, among whom were also Communists. The meeting was opened by the sailor Petrichenko, and a *Presidium* (Executive Committee) of five members was elected *viva voce*. The main question before the delegates was the approaching new elections to the Kronstadt Soviet to be based on more equitable principles than heretofore. The meeting was also to take action on the Resolutions of March 1, and to consider ways and means of helping the country out of the desperate condition created by famine and fuel shortage.

The spirit of the Conference was thoroughly Sovietist; Kronstadt demanded Soviets free from interference by any political party; it wanted non-partisan Soviets that should truly reflect the needs and express the will of the workers and peasants. The attitude of the delegates was antagonistic to the arbitrary rule of bureaucratic commissars, but friendly to the Communist Party as such. They were staunch adherents of the Soviet **system** and they were earnestly seeking to find, by means friendly and peaceful, a solution of the pressing problems.

Kuzmin, Commissar of the Baltic Fleet, was the first to address the Conference. A man of more energy than judgement, he entirely failed to grasp the great significance of the moment. He was not equal to the situation; he did not know how to reach the hearts and minds of those simple men, the sailors and workers who had sacrificed so much for the Revolution and who were now exhausted to the point of desperation. The delegates had gathered to take counsel with the representatives of the Government. Instead, Kuzmin's speech proved a firebrand thrown into gunpowder. He incensed the Conference by his arrogance and insolence. He denied the labour disorders in Petrograd, declaring that the city was quiet and the workers satisfied. He praised the work of the Commissars, questioned the revolutionary motives of Kronstadt and warned against danger from Poland. He stooped to unworthy insinuations and thundered threats. 'If you want open warfare', Kuzmin concluded,'you shall have it, for the Communists will not give up the reins of government. We will fight to the bitter end.'

This tactless and provoking speech of the Commissar of the Baltic Fleet served to insult and outrage the delegates. The address of the Chairman of the Kronstadt Soviet, the Communist Vassiliev, who was the next speaker, made no impression on the audience; the man was colourless and indefinite. As the meeting progressed, the general attitude became more clearly anti-Bolshevik. Still the delegates were hoping to reach some friendly understanding with the representatives of the Government. But presently it became apparent, states the official report,* that 'we could not trust comrades Kuzmin and Vassiliev any more, and that it was necessary to detain them temporarily, especially because the Communists were in possession of arms, and we had no access to the telephones. The soldiers stood in fear of the Commissars, as proved by the letter read at the meeting, and the

* *Izvestia* of the Provisional Revolutionary Committee of Kronstadt, Number 9, March 11,1921.

Communists did not permit gatherings of the garrison to take place.'

Kuzmin and Vassiliev were therefore removed from the meeting and placed under arrest. It is characteristic of the spirit of the Conference that the motion to detain the other Communists present was voted down by an overwhelming majority. The delegates held that the Communists must be considered on equal footing with the representatives of other organisations and accorded the same rights and treatment. Kronstadt still was determined to find some bond of agreement with the Communist Party and the Bolshevik Government.

The Resolutions of March 1 were read and enthusiastically passed. At that moment the Conference was thrown into great excitement by the declaration of a delegate that the Bolsheviks were about to attack the meeting and that fifteen carloads of soldiers and Communists, armed with rifles and machine guns, had been dispatched for that purpose. 'This information', the *Izvestia* report continues, 'produced passionate resentment among the delegates. Investigation soon proved the report groundless, but rumours persisted that a regiment of *kursanti*, headed by the notorious Chekist Dulkiss, was already marching in the direction of the fort Krasnaia Gorka'. In view of these new developments, and remembering the threats of Kuzmin and Kalinin, the Conference at once took up the question of organising the defence of Kronstadt against Bolshevik attack. Time pressing, it was decided to turn the *Presidium* of the Conference into a Provisional Revolutionary Committee, which was charged with preserving the order and safety of the city. That Committee was also to make the necessary preparations for holding the new elections to the Kronstadt Soviet.

3   Bolshevik Conspiracy Against Kronstadt

Petrograd was in a state of high nervous tension. New strikes had broken out and there were persistent rumours of labour disorders in Moscow, of peasant uprisings in the East and in Siberia. For lack of a reliable public press the people gave credence to the most exaggerated and even to obviously false reports. All eyes were on Kronstadt in expectation of momentous developments.

The Bolsheviks lost no time in organising their attack against Kronstadt. Already on March 2 the Government issued a *prikaz* (order) signed by Lenin and Trotsky, which denounced the Kronstadt movement as a *myatezh*, a mutiny against the Communist authorities. In that document the sailors were charged with being 'the tools of former Tsarist generals who together with Socialist Revolutionist traitors staged a counter-revolutionary conspiracy against the proletarian

Republic'. The Kronstadt movement for free Soviets was characterised by Lenin and Trotsky as 'the work of Entente interventionists and French spies'. 'On February 28', the *prikaz* read, 'there were passed by the men of the *Petropavlovsk* resolutions breathing the spirit of the Black Hundreds. Then there appeared on the scene the group of the former general, Kozlovsky. He and three of his officers, whose names we have not yet ascertained, have openly assumed the role of rebellion. Thus the meaning of recent events has become evident. Behind the Socialist Revolutionists again stands a Tsarist general. In view of all this the Council of Labour and Defence orders -

1) To declare the former general Kozlovsky and his aides outlawed;

2) To put the City of Petrograd and the Petrograd Province under martial law;

3) To place supreme power over the whole Petrograd District into the hands of the Petrograd Defence Committee'.

There was indeed a former general, Kozlovsky, in Kronstadt. It was Trotsky who had placed him there as an artillery specialist. He played no role whatever in the Kronstadt events, but the Bolsheviks cleverly exploited his name to denounce the sailors as enemies of the Soviet Republic and their movement as counter-revolutionary. The official Bolshevik press now began its campaign of calumny and defamation of Kronstadt as a hotbed of 'White conspiracy headed by General Kozlovsky', and Communist agitators were sent among the workers in the mills and factories of Petrograd and Moscow to call upon the proletariat 'to rally to the support and defence of the Workers' and Peasants' Government against the counter-revolutionary uprising in Kronstadt'.

Far from having anything to do with generals and counter-revolutionists, the Kronstadt sailors refused to accept aid even from the Socialist Revolutionist Party. Its leader, Victor Chernov, then in Reval, attempted to influence the sailors in favour of his Party and its demands, but received no encouragement from the Provisional Revolutionary Committee. Chernov sent to Kronstadt the following radio*-

> The Chairman of the Constituent Assembly, Victor Chernov, sends his fraternal greetings to the heroic comrades-sailors, the Red Army men and workers, who for the third time since 1905 are throwing off the yoke of tyranny. He offers to aid with men and to provision Kronstadt through the Russian co-operatives

*Published in Revolutsionaya Rossiya (Socialist Revolutionist journal), Number 8, May 1921. See also Moscow *Izvestia* (Communist), Number 154, July 13, 1922.

abroad. Inform what and how much is needed. Am prepared to come in person and give my energies and authority to the service of the people's revolution. I have faith in the final victory of the labouring masses....Hail to the first to raise the banner of the people's liberation! Down with despotism from the left and right!

At the same time the Socialist Revolutionary Party sent the following message to Kronstadt;

The Socialist Revolutionist delegation abroad....now that the cup of the people's wrath is overflowing, offers to help with all means in its power in the struggle for liberty and popular government. Inform in what ways help is desired. Long live the people's revolution! Long live free Soviets and the Constituent Assembly!

The Kronstadt Revolutionary Committee declined the Socialist Revolutionist offers. It sent the following reply to Victor Chernov;

The Provisional Revolutionary Committee of Kronstadt expresses to all our brothers abroad its deep gratitude and sympathy. The Provisional Revolutionary Committee is thankful for the offer of comrade Chernov, but it refrains for the present; that is, till further developments become clarified. Meantime, everything will be taken into consideration.

Petrichenko
Chairman Provisional Revolutionary Committee

Moscow, however, continued its campaign of misrepresentation. On March 3 the Bolshevik radio sent out the following message to the world (certain parts undecipherable owing to interference from another station);

....That the armed uprising of the former general Kozlovsky has been organised by the spies of the Entente, like many similar previous plots, is evident from the bourgeois French newspaper *Matin*, which two weeks prior to the Kozlovsky rebellion published the following telegram from Helsingfors; 'As a result of the recent Kronstadt uprising the Bolshevik military authorities have taken steps to isolate Kronstadt and to prevent the sailors and soldiers of Kronstadt from entering Petrograd'....It is clear that the Kronstadt uprising was made in Paris and organised by the French secret service....The Socialist Revolutionists, also controlled and directed from Paris, have been preparing rebellions against the Soviet Government, and no sooner were their preparations made than there appeared the real master, the Tsarist general.

The character of the numerous other messages sent by Moscow can be judged by the following radio;

Petrograd is orderly and quiet, and even the few factories where accusations against the Soviet Government were recently voiced now understand that it is the work of provocateurs. They realise where the agents of the Entente and of counter-revolution are leading them to.

....Just at this moment, when in America a new republican regime is assuming the reins of government and showing inclination to take up business relations with Soviet Russia, the spreading of lying rumours and the organisation of disturbances in Kronstadt have the sole purpose of influencing the new American President and changing his policy toward Russia. At the same time the London Conference is holding its sessions, and the spreading of similar rumours must influence also the Turkish delegation and make it more submissive to the demands of the Entente. The rebellion of the *Petropavlovsk* crew is undoubtedly part of a great conspiracy to create trouble within Soviet Russia and to injure our international position....This plan is being carried out within Russia by a Tsarist general and former officers, and their activities are supported by the Mensheviks and Socialist Revolutionists.

The Petrograd Committee of Defence, directed by Zinoviev, its Chairman, assumed full control of the City and Province of Petrograd. The whole Northern District was put under martial law and all meetings prohibited. Extraordinary precautions were taken to protect the Government institutions and machine guns were placed in the Astoria, the hotel occupied by Zinoviev and other high Bolshevik functionaries. The proclamations pasted on the street bulletin boards ordered the immediate return of all strikers to the factories, prohibited suspension of work, and warned the people against congregating on the streets. 'In such cases', the order read, 'the soldiery will resort to arms. In case of resistance, shooting on the spot'.

The Committee of Defence took up the systematic 'cleaning of the city'. Numerous workers, soldiers and sailors, suspected of sympathising with Kronstadt, were placed under arrest. All Petrograd sailors and several Army regiments thought to be 'politically untrustworthy' were ordered to distant points, while the families of Kronstadt sailors living in Petrograd were taken into custody **as hostages**. The Committee of Defence notified Kronstadt of its action by a proclamation scattered over the city from an aeroplane on March 4, which stated;

The Committee of Defence declares that the arrested are held as hostages for the Commissar of the Baltic Fleet, N.N.Kuzmin, the Chairman of the Kronstadt Soviet, T.Vassiliev, and other Communists. If the least harm be suffered by our detained comrades, the hostages will pay with their lives.

'We do not want bloodshed. Not a single Communist has been shot by us', was Kronstadt's reply.

4   The Aims of Kronstadt

Kronstadt revived with new life. Revolutionary enthusiasm rose to the level of the October days when the heroism and devotion of the sailors played such a decisive role. Now, for the first time since the Communist Party assumed exclusive control of the Revolution and the fate of Russia, Kronstadt felt itself free. A new spirit of solidarity and brotherhood brought the sailors, the soldiers of the garrison, the factory workers, and the non-partisan elements together in united effort for their common cause. Even Communists were infected by the fraternisation of the whole city and joined in the work preparatory to the approaching elections to the Kronstadt Soviet.

Among the first steps taken by the Provisional Revolutionary Committee was the preservation of revolutionary order in Kronstadt and the publication of the Committee's official organ, the daily *Izvestia*. Its first appeal to the people of Kronstadt (issue number 1, March 3, 1921) was thoroughly characteristic of the attitude and temper of the sailors. 'The Revolutionary Committee', it read, 'is most concerned that no blood be shed. It has exerted its best efforts to organise revolutionary order in the city, the fortress and the forts. Comrades and citizens, do not suspend work! Workers, remain at your machines; sailors and soldiers, be on your posts. All Soviet employees and institutions should continue their labours. The Provisional Revolutionary Committee calls upon you all, comrades and citizens, to give it your support and aid. Its mission is to organise, in fraternal co-operation with you, the conditions necessary for honest and just elections to the new Soviet'.

The pages of the *Izvestia* bear abundant witness to the deep faith of the Revolutionary Committee in the people of Kronstadt and their aspirations towards free Soviets as the true road of liberation from the oppression of Communist bureaucracy. In its daily organ and radio messages the Revolutionary Committee indignantly resented the Bolshevik campaign of calumny and repeatedly appealed to the proletariat of Russia and of the world for understanding, sympathy, and help. The radio of March 6 sounds the keynote of Kronstadt's call;

Our cause is just: we stand for the power of Soviets, not parties. We stand for freely elected representatives of the labouring masses. The substitute Soviets manipulated by the Communist Party have always been deaf to our needs and demands; the only reply we have ever received was shooting....Comrades! They not only deceive you: they deliberately pervert the truth and resort to most despicable defamation....In Kronstadt the whole power is exclusively in the hands of the revolutionary sailors, soldiers and workers - not with counter-revolutionists led by some Kozlovsky, as the lying Moscow radio tries to make you believe....Do not delay, comrades! Join us, get in touch with us: demand admission to Kronstadt for your delegates. Only they will tell you the whole truth and will expose the fiendish calumny about Finnish bread and Entente offers.

Long live the revolutionary proletariat and the peasantry!

Long live the power of freely elected Soviets!

The Provisional Revolutionary Committee first had its headquarters on the flagship *Petropavlovsk*, but within a few days it removed to the 'People's Home', in the centre of Kronstadt, in order to be, as the *Izvestia* states, 'in closer touch with the people and make access to the Committee easier than on the ship'. Although the Communist press continued its virulent denunciation of Kronstadt as 'the counter-revolutionary rebellion of General Kozlovsky', the truth of the matter was that the Revolutionary Committee was exclusively proletarian, consisting for the most part of workers of known revolutionary record. The Committee comprised the following 15 members:

1) Petrichenko, senior clerk, flagship *Petropavlovsk*
2) Yakovenko, telephone operator, Kronstadt District
3) Ossossov, machinist, *Sevastopol*
4) Arkhipov, engineer
5) Perepelkin, mechanic, *Sevastopol*
6) Patrushev, head mechanic, *Petropavlovsk*
7) Kupolov, senior medical assistant
8) Vershinin, sailor, *Sevastopol*
9) Tukin, electrical mechanic
10) Romanenko, caretaker of aviation docks
11) Oreshin, manager of the Third Industrial School
12) Valk, lumber mill worker
13) Pavlov, naval mining worker
14) Baikov, carter
15) Kilgast, deep sea sailor.

Not without a sense of humour did the Kronstadt *Izvestia* remark in this connection; 'These are **our** generals, Messrs. Trotsky and Zinoviev, while the Brussilovs, the Kamenevs, the Tukhachevskis, and the other celebrities of the Tsarist regime are on **your** side'.

The Provisional Revolutionary Committee enjoyed the confidence of the whole population of Kronstadt. It won general respect by establishing and firmly adhering to the principle of 'equal rights for all, privileges to none'. The *payok* (food ration) was equalised. The sailors, who under Bolshevik rule always received rations far in excess of those allotted to the workers, themselves voted to accept no more than the average citizen and toiler. Special rations and delicacies were given only to hospitals and children's homes.

The just and generous attitude of the Revolutionary Committee toward the Kronstadt members of the Communist Party - few of whom had been arrested in spite of Bolshevik repressions and the holding of the sailors' families as hostages - won the respect even of the Communists. The pages of the *Izvestia* contain numerous communications from Communist groups and organisations of Kronstadt, condemning the attitude of the Central Government and endorsing the stand and measures of the Provisional Revolutionary Committee. Many Kronstadt Communists publicly announced their withdrawal from the Party as a protest against its despotism and bureaucratic corruption. In various issues of the *Izvestia* there are to be found hundreds of names of Communists whose conscience made it impossible for them to 'remain in the Party of the executioner Trotsky', as some of them expressed it. Resignations from the Communist Party soon became so numerous as to resemble a general exodus.* The following letters, taken at random from a large batch, sufficiently characterise the sentiment of the Kronstadt Communists;

(1)

I have come to realise that the policies of the Communist Party have brought the country into a hopeless blind alley from which there is no exit. The Party has become bureaucratic, it has learned nothing and it does not want to learn. It refuses to listen to the voice of 115 million peasants; it does not want to consider that only freedom of speech and opportunity to participate in the reconstruction of the country, by means of altered election methods, can bring our country out of its lethargy.

I refuse henceforth to consider myself a member of the Russian Communist Party. I wholly approve of the resolution passed by

*The Executive Committee of the Communist Party of Russia considered its Kronstadt section so 'demoralised' that after the defeat of Kronstadt it ordered a complete de-registration of all Kronstadt Communists. (A. B.)

the all-city meeting on March 1, and I hereby place my energies and abilities at the disposal of the Provisional Revolutionary Committee.

Herman Kanev
Krasniy Komandir (Red Army Officer)
Son of the political exile in the Trial of 193*
Izvestia, number 3, March 5, 1921

(2)

Comrades, my pupils of the Industrial Red Army, and Naval Schools!

Almost thirty years have I lived in deep love of the people, and have carried light and knowledge, so far as lay in my power, to all who thirsted for it, up to the present moment.

The Revolution of 1917 gave greater scope to my work, increased my activities, and I devoted myself with greater energy to the service of my ideal.

The Communist slogan, 'All for the people', inspired me with its nobility and beauty, and in February, 1920, I entered the Russian Communist Party as a candidate. But the 'first shot' fired at the peaceful population, at my dearly beloved children of which there are about seven thousand in Kronstadt, fills me with horror that I may be considered as sharing responsibility for the blood of the innocents thus shed. I feel that I can no longer believe in and propagate that which has disgraced itself by a fiendish act. Therefore with the first shot I have ceased to regard myself as a member of the Communist Party.

Maria Nikolayevna Shatel
Teacher

Izvestia, number 6, March 8, 1921

Such communications appeared in almost every issue of the *Izvestia*. Most significant was the declaration of the Provisional Bureau of the Kronstadt Section of the Communist Party, whose manifesto to its members was published in the *Izvestia*, number 2, March 4;

....Let every comrade of our Party realise the importance of the present hour.

Give no credence to the false rumours that Communists are being shot, and that the Kronstadt Communists are about to rise up in arms. Such rumours are spread to cause bloodshed.

We declare that our Party has always been defending the con-

---

*The celebrated trial of 193 in the early days of the revolutionary movement of Russia. It began in the latter part of 1877, closing in the first months of 1878. (A. B.)

quests of the working class against all known and secret enemies of the power of the workers' and peasants' Soviets, and will continue to do so.

The Provisional Bureau of the Kronstadt Communist Party recognises the necessity for new elections to the Soviet and calls upon the members of the Communist Party to take part in the elections.

The Provisional Bureau of the Communist Party directs all members of the Party to remain at their posts and in no way to obstruct or interfere with the measures of the Provisional Revolutionary Committee.

Long live the power of the Soviets!

Long live the international union of workers!

Provisional Bureau of the Kronstadt Section
of the Russian Communist Party
F. Pervushin
Y. Ylyin
A. Kabanov

Similarly various other organisations, civil and military, expressed their opposition to the Moscow regime and their entire agreement with the demands of the Kronstadt sailors. Many resolutions to that effect were also passed by Red Army regiments stationed in Kronstadt and on duty in the forts. The following is expressive of their general spirit and tendency;

We, Red Army soldiers of the fort *Krasnoarmeetz*, stand wholly with the Provisional Revolutionary Committee, and to the last moment we will defend the Revolutionary Committee, the workers and the peasants.

....Let no one believe the lies of the Communist proclamations thrown from aeroplanes. We have no generals here and no Tsarist officers. Kronstadt has always been the city of workers and peasants and so it will remain. The generals are in the service of the Communists.

....At this moment, when the fate of the country is in the balance, we who have taken the power into our own hands and who have entrusted the Revolutionary Committee with leadership in the fight - we declare to the whole garrison and to the workers that we are prepared to die for the liberty of the labouring masses. Freed from the three year old Communist yoke and terror we shall die rather than recede a single step. Long live Free Russia of the Working People!

Crew of the Fort *Krasnoarmeetz*
Izvestia, number 5, March 7, 1921

Kronstadt was inspired by passionate love of a Free Russia and unbounded faith in true Soviets. It was confident of gaining the support of the whole of Russia, of Petrograd in particular, thus bringing about the final liberation of the country. The Kronstadt *Izvestia* reiterates this hope and attitude, and in numerous articles and appeals it seeks to clarify its position toward the Bolsheviks and its aspiration to lay the foundation of a new, free life for itself and the rest of Russia. This great aspiration, the purity of its motives, and its fervent hope of liberation stand out in striking relief on the pages of the official organ of the Kronstadt Provisional Revolutionary Committee and thoroughly express the spirit of the soldiers, sailors and workers. The virulent attacks of the Bolshevik press, the infamous lies sent broadcast by the Moscow radio station accusing Kronstadt of counter- revolution and White conspiracy, the Revolutionary Committee replied to in a dignified manner. It often reproduced in its organ the Moscow proclamations in order to show to the people of Kronstadt to what depths the Bolsheviks had sunk. Occasionally the Communist methods were exposed and characterised by the *Izvestia* with just indignation, as in its issue of March 8, (number 6), under the heading 'We and They';

Not knowing how to retain the power that is falling from their hands, the Communists resort to the vilest provocative means. Their contemptible press has mobilised all its forces to incite the masses and put the Kronstadt movement in the light of a White guard conspiracy. Now a clique of shameless villians has sent word to the world that 'Kronstadt has sold itself to Finland'. Their newspapers spit fire and poison, and because they have failed to persuade the proletariat that Kronstadt is in the hands of counter-revolutionists, they are now trying to play on the nationalistic feelings.

The whole world already knows from our radios what the Kronstadt garrison and workers are fighting for. But the Communists are striving to pervert the meaning of events and thus mislead our Petrograd brothers.

Petrograd is surrounded by the bayonets of the *kursanti* and the Party 'guards', and Maliuta Skuratov - Trotsky - does not permit the delegates of the non-partisan workers and soldiers to go to Kronstadt. He fears they would learn the whole truth there, and that truth would immediately sweep the Communists away and the thus enlightened labouring masses would take the power into their own horny hands.

That is the reason that the *Petro-Soviet* (Soviet of Petrograd) did not reply to our radio-telegram in which we asked that really impartial comrades be sent to Kronstadt.

Fearing for their own skins, the leaders of the Communists suppress the truth and disseminate the lie that White guardists are active in Kronstadt, that the Kronstadt proletariat has sold itself to Finland and to French spies, that the Finns have already organised an army in order to attack Petrograd with the aid of the Kronstadt *myatezhniki* (mutineers), and so forth.

To all this we can reply only this; All power to the Soviets! Keep your hands off them, the hands that are red with the blood of the martyrs of liberty who have died fighting against the White guardists, the landlords, and the bourgeoisie!

In simple and frank speech Kronstadt sought to express the will of the people yearning for freedom and for the opportunity to shape their own destinies. It felt itself the advance guard, so to speak, of the proletariat of Russia about to rise in defence of the great aspirations for which the people had fought and suffered in the October Revolution. The faith of Kronstadt in the Soviet system was deep and firm; its all-inclusive slogan, **All power to the Soviets, not to parties!** That was its programme; it did not have time to develop it or to theorise. It strove for the emancipation of the people from the Communist yoke. That yoke, no longer bearable, made a new revolution, the **Third Revolution**, necessary. The road to liberty and peace lay in freely elected Soviets, 'the cornerstone of the new revolution'. The pages of the *Izvestia* bear rich testimony to the unspoiled directness and single-mindedness of the Kronstadt sailors and workers, and the touching faith they had in their mission as the initiators of the Third Revolution. These aspirations and hopes are clearly set forth in number 6 of the *Izvestia*, March 8, in the leading editorial entitled 'What We Are Fighting For';

With the October Revolution the working class had hoped to achieve its emancipation. But there resulted an even greater enslavement of human personality.

The power of the police and gendarme monarchy fell into the hands of usurpers - the Communists - who, instead of giving the people liberty, have instilled in them only the constant fear of the Cheka, which by its horrors surpasses even the gendarme regime of Tsarism....Worse and most criminal of all is the spiritual cabal of the Communists: they have laid their hand also on the internal world of the labouring masses, compelling everyone to think according to Communist prescription.

....Russia of the toilers, the first to raise the red banner of labour's emancipation, is drenched with the blood of those martyred for the greater glory of Communist dominion. In that sea of blood the Communists are drowning all the bright promises and possibilities of the workers' revolution. It has now become clear that the

Russian Communist Party is not the defender of the labouring masses, as it pretends to be. The interests of the working people are foreign to it. Having gained power it is now fearful only of losing it, and therefore it considers all means permissible: defamation, deceit, violence, murder, and vengeance upon the families of the rebels.

There is an end to long-suffering patience. Here and there the land is lit up by the fires of rebellion in a struggle against oppression and violence. Strikes of workers have multiplied, but the Bolshevik police regime has taken every precaution against the outbreak of the inevitable Third Revolution.

But in spite of it all it has come, and it is made by the hands of the labouring masses. The Generals of Communism see clearly that it is the people who have risen, the people who have become convinced that the Communists have betrayed the ideas of Socialism. Fearing for their safety and knowing that there is no place they can hide in from the wrath of the workers, the Communists still try to terrorise the rebels with prison, shooting, and other barbarities.But life under the Communist dictatorship is more terrible than death...

There is no middle road. To conquer or to die! The example is being set by Kronstadt, the terror of counter-revolution from the right and from the left. Here has taken place the great revolutionary deed. Here is raised the banner of rebellion against the three year old tyranny and oppression of Communist autocracy, which has put in the shade the three hundred year old despotism of monarchism. Here, in Kronstadt, has been laid the cornerstone of the Third Revolution which is to break the last chains of the worker and open the new, broad road to Socialist creativeness.

This new Revolution will rouse the masses of the East and the West, and it will serve as an example of new Socialist constructiveness, in contradistinction to the governmental, cut and dried Communist 'construction'. The labouring masses will learn that what has been done till now in the name of the workers and peasants was not Socialism.

Without firing a single shot, without shedding a drop of blood, the first step has been taken. Those who labour need no blood. They will shed it only in self-defence....The workers and peasants march on: they are leaving behind them the *utchredilka* (Constituent Assembly) with its bourgeois regime and the Communist Party dictatorship with its Cheka and State capitalism, which have put the noose around the neck of the workers and threaten to strangle them to death.

The present change offers the labouring masses the opportunity of securing, at last, freely elected Soviets which will function without fear of the Party whip; they can now re-organise the governmentalised labour unions into voluntary associations of workers, peasants, and the working intelligentsia. At last is broken the police club of Communist autocracy.

That was the programme, those the immediate demands, for which the Bolshevik government began the attack of Kronstadt at 6 - 45 p.m., March 7, 1921.

5 Bolshevik Ultimatum to Kronstadt

Kronstadt was generous. Not a drop of Communist blood did it shed, in spite of all the provocation, the blockade of the city and the repressive measures on the part of the Bolshevik Government. It scorned to imitate the Communist example of vengeance, even going to the extent of warning the Kronstadt population not to be guilty of excesses against members of the Communist Party. The Provisional Revolutionary Committee issued a call to the people of Kronstadt to that effect, even after the Bolshevik Government had ignored the demand of the sailors for the liberation of the hostages taken in Petrograd. The Kronstadt demand sent by radio to the Petrograd Soviet and the Manifesto of the Revolutionary Committee were published on the same day, March 7, and are hereby reproduced;

In the name of the Kronstadt garrison the Provisional Revolutionary Committee of Kronstadt demands that the families of the sailors, workers and Red Army men held by the *Petro-Soviet* as hostages be liberated within 24 hours.

The Kronstadt garrison declares that the Communists enjoy full liberty in Kronstadt and their families are absolutely safe. The example of the *Petro-Soviet* will not be followed here, because we consider such methods (the taking of hostages) most shameful and vicious even if prompted by desperate fury. History knows no such infamy.

Sailor Petrichenko
Chairman Provisional Revolutionary Committee
Kilgast
Secretary

The Manifesto to the people of Kronstadt read in part;

The long continued oppression of the labouring masses by the Communist dictatorship has produced very natural indignation and resentment on the part of the people. As a result of it relatives of Communists have in some instances been discharged from their positions and boycotted. That must not be. **We do not seek vengeance - we are defending our labour interests.**

Kronstadt lived in the spirit of its holy crusade. It had abiding faith in the justice of its cause and felt itself the true defender of the Revolution. In this state of mind the sailors did not believe that the Government would attack them by force of arms. In the subconsciousness of these simple children of the soil and sea there perhaps germinated the feeling that **not only through violence may victory be gained**. The Slavic psychology seemed to believe that the justice of the cause and the strength of revolutionary spirit must win. At any rate, Kronstadt refused to take the offensive. The Revolutionary Committee would not accept the insistent advice of the military experts to make an immediate landing in Oranienbaum, a fort of great strategic value. The Kronstadt sailors and soldiers aimed to establish free Soviets and were willing to defend their rights against attack; but they would not be the aggressors.

In Petrograd there were persistent rumours that the Government was preparing military operations against Kronstadt, but the people did not credit such stories; the thing seemed so outrageous as to be absurd. As already mentioned, the Committee of Defence (officially known as the Soviet of Labour and Defence) had declared the capital to be in an 'extraordinary state of siege'. No assemblies were permitted, no gathering on the streets. The Petrograd workers knew little of what was transpiring in Kronstadt, the only information accessible being the Communist press and the frequent bulletins to the effect that the 'Tsarist General Kozlovsky organised a counter-revolutionary uprising in Kronstadt'. Anxiously the people looked forward to the announced session of the Petrograd Soviet which was to take action in the Kronstadt matter.

The *Petro-Soviet* met on March 4, admission being by cards which, as a rule, only Communists could procure. The writer, then on friendly terms with the Bolsheviks and particularly with Zinoviev, was present. As chairman of the Petrograd Soviet Zinoviev opened the session and in a long speech set forth the Kronstadt situation. I confess that I came to the meeting disposed rather in favour of the Zinoviev viewpoint; I was on my guard against the vaguest possibility of counter-revolutionary influence in Kronstadt. But Zinoviev's speech itself convinced me that the Communist accusations against the sailors were pure fabrication, without a scintilla of truth. I had heard Zinoviev on several previous occasions. I found him a convincing speaker, once his premises were admitted. But now his whole attitude, his argumentation, his tone and manner - all gave the lie to his words. I could sense his own conscience protesting. The only 'evidence' presented against Kronstadt was the famous resolution of March 1, the demands of

81

which were just and even moderate. Yet it was on the sole basis of that document, supported by the vehement, almost hysterical denunciation of the sailors by Kalinin, that the fatal step was taken. Prepared beforehand and presented by the stentorian-voiced Yevdokimov, the right-hand man of Zinoviev, the resolution against Kronstadt was passed by the delegates wrought up to a high pitch of intolerance and blood thirst - passed amid a tumult of protest from several delegates of Petrograd factories and the spokesmen of the sailors. The resolution declared Kronstadt guilty of a counter-revolutionary uprising against the Soviet power and demanded its immediate surrender.

It was a declaration of war. Even many Communists refused to believe that the resolution would be carried out; it were a monstrous thing to attack by force of arms the 'pride and glory of the Russian Revolution', as Trotsky had christened the Kronstadt sailors. In the circle of their friends many sober-minded Communists threatened to resign from the Party should such a bloody deed come to pass.

Trotsky had been expected to address the *Petro-Soviet*, and his failure to appear was interpreted by some as indicating that the seriousness of the situation was exaggerated. But during the night he arrived in Petrograd and the following morning, March 5, he issued his ultimatum to Kronstadt;

> The Workers' and Peasants' Government has decreed that Kronstadt and the rebellious ships must immediately submit to the authority of the Soviet Republic. Therefore I command all who have raised their hand against the Socialist fatherland to lay down their arms at once. The obdurate are to be disarmed and turned over to the Soviet authorities. The arrested Commissars and other representatives of the Government are to liberated at once. Only those surrendering unconditionally may count on the mercy of the Soviet Republic.
>
> Simultaneously I am issuing orders to prepare to quell the mutiny and subdue the mutineers by force of arms. Responsibility for the harm that may be suffered by the peaceful population will fall entirely upon the heads of the counter-revolutionary mutineers.
>
> This warning is final.
>
> Trotsky
> Chairman Revolutionary Military Soviet of the Republic
> Kamenev
> Commander-in-Chief

The situation looked ominous. Great military forces continuously flowed into Petrograd and its environs. Trotsky's ultimatum was followed by a *prikaz* which contained the historic threat, 'I'll shoot you like pheasants'. A group of Anarchists then in Petrograd made a last attempt to induce the Bolsheviks to reconsider their decision of attacking Kronstadt. They felt it their duty to the Revolution to make an effort, even if hopeless, to prevent the imminent massacre of the revolutionary flower of Russia, the Kronstadt sailors and workers. On March 5 they sent a peaceful protest to the Committee of Defence, pointing out the peaceful intentions and just demands of Kronstadt, reminding the Communists of the heroic revolutionary history of the sailors, and suggesting a method of settling the dispute in a manner befitting comrades and revolutionists. The document read;

To the Petrograd Soviet of Labour and Defence
Chairman Zinoviev

To remain silent **now** is impossible, even criminal. Recent events impel us Anarchists to speak out and to declare our attitude in the present situation.

The spirit of ferment and dissatisfaction manifest among the workers and sailors is the result of causes that demand our serious attention. Cold and hunger have produced disaffection, and the absence of any opportunity for discussion and criticism is forcing the workers and sailors to air their grievances in the open.

White-guardist bands wish and may try to exploit this dissatisfaction in their own class interests. Hiding behind the workers and sailors they throw out slogans of the Constituent Assembly, of free trade, and similar demands.

We Anarchists have long ago exposed the fiction of these slogans, and we declare to the whole world that we will fight with arms against any counter-revolutionary attempt, in co-operation with all friends of the Social Revolution and hand in hand with the Bolsheviks.

Concerning the conflict between the Soviet Government and the workers and sailors, we hold that it must be settled not by force of arms but by means of comradely, fraternal revolutionary agreement. Resorting to bloodshed, on the part of the Soviet Government, will not - in the given situation - intimidate or quieten the workers. On the contrary, it will serve only to aggravate matters and will strengthen the hands of the Entente and of internal counter-revolution.

More important still, the use of force by the Workers' and Peasants' Government against workers and sailors will have a reactionary effect upon the international revolutionary movement and will everywhere result in incalculable harm to the Social Revolution.

Comrade Bolsheviks, bethink yourselves before it is too late! Do not play with fire: you are about to make a most serious and decisive step.

We hereby submit to you the following proposition: Let a

83

Commission be selected to consist of five persons, inclusive of two
Anarchists. The Commission is to go to Kronstadt to settle the
dispute by peaceful means. In the given situation this is the most
radical method. It will be of international revolutionary significance.

Petrograd, March 5, 1921
Alexander Berkman
Emma Goldman
Perkus
Petrovsky

Zinoviev, informed that a document in connection with the Kronstadt problem was to be submitted to the Soviet of Defence, sent his personal representative for it. Whether the letter was discussed by that body is not known to the writer. At any rate, no action was taken in the matter.

6   The First Shot

Kronstadt, heroic and generous, was dreaming of liberating Russia by the Third Revolution which it felt proud to have initiated. It formulated no definite programme. Liberty and universal brotherhood were its slogans. It thought of the Third Revolution as a gradual process of emancipation, the first step in that direction being the free election of independent Soviets, uncontrolled by any political party and expressive of the will and interests of the people. The whole-hearted, unsophisticated sailors were proclaiming to the workers of the world their great Ideal, and calling upon the proletariat to join forces in the common fight, confident that their Cause would find enthusiastic support and that the workers of Petrograd, first and foremost, would hasten to their aid.

Meanwhile Trotsky had collected his forces. The most trusted divisions from the fronts, *kursanti* regiments, Cheka detachments, and military units consisting exclusively of Communists were now gathered in the forts of Sestroretsk, Lissy Noss, Krasnaia Gorka, and neighbouring fortified places. The greatest Russian military experts were rushed to the scene to form plans for the blockade and attack of Kronstadt, and the notorious Tukhachevski was appointed Commander-in-Chief in the siege of Kronstadt.

On March 7, at 6.45 in the evening, the Communist batteries of Sestroretsk and Lissy Noss fired the first shots against Kronstadt.

It was the anniversary of the Women Workers' Day. Kronstadt, besieged and attacked, did not forget the great holiday. Under fire of numerous batteries, the brave sailors sent a radio greeting to the

84

working-women of the world, an act most characteristic of the psychology of the Rebel City. The radio read;

> Today is a universal holiday - Women Workers' Day. We of Kronstadt send, amid the thunder of cannon, our fraternal greetings to the working-women of the world....May you soon accomplish your liberation from every form of violence and oppression. ....Long live the free revolutionary working-women! Long live the Social Revolution throughout the world!

No less characteristic was the heart-rending cry of Kronstadt, 'Let The Whole World Know', published after the first shot had been fired, in number 6 of the *Izvestia*, March 8;

> The first shot has been fired....Standing up to his knees in the blood of the workers, Marshal Trotsky was the first to open fire against revolutionary Kronstadt which has risen against the autocracy of the Communists to establish the true power of the Soviets.
>
> Without shedding a drop of blood we, Red Army men, sailors, and workers of Kronstadt have freed ourselves from the yoke of the Communists and have even preserved their lives. By the threat of artillery they want now to subject us again to their tyranny.
>
> Not wishing bloodshed, we asked that non-partisan delegates of the Petrograd proletariat be sent to us, that they may learn that Kronstadt is fighting for the Power of the Soviets. But the Communists have kept our demand from the workers of Petrograd and now they have opened fire - the usual reply of the pseudo Workers' and Peasants' Government to the demands of the labouring masses.
>
> Let the workers of the whole world know that we, the defenders of Soviet Power, are guarding the conquests of the Social Revolution.
>
> We will win or perish beneath the ruins of Kronstadt, fighting for the just cause of the labouring masses.
>
> The workers of the world will be our judges. The blood of the innocent will fall upon the heads of the Communist fanatics drunk with authority.
>
> Long live the Power of the Soviets!

7   The Defeat of Kronstadt

The artillery bombardment of Kronstadt, which began on the evening of March 7, was followed by the attempt to take the fortress by storm. The attack was made from the north and the south by picked Comminist troops clad in white shrouds, the colour of which protectively blended with the snow lying thick on the frozen Gulf of

Finland. These first terrible attempts to take the fortress by storm, at the reckless sacrifice of life, are mourned by the sailors in touching commiseration for their brothers in arms, duped into believing Kronstadt counter-revolutionary. Under date of March 8 the Kronstadt *Izvestia* wrote;

> We did not want to shed the blood of our brothers, and we did not fire a single shot until compelled to do so. We had to defend the just cause of the labouring people and to shoot - to shoot at our own brothers sent to certain death by Communists who have grown fat at the expense of the people.
>
> ....To your misfortune there broke a terrific snowstorm and black night shrouded everything in darkness. Nevertheless, the Communist executioners, counting no cost, drove you along the ice, threatening you in the rear with their machine guns operated by Communist detachments.
>
> Many of you perished that night on the icy vastness of the Gulf of Finland. And when day broke and the storm quieted down, only pitiful remnants of you, worn and hungry, hardly able to move, came to us clad in your white shrouds.
>
> Early in the morning there were already about a thousand of you and later in the day a countless number. Dearly you have paid with your blood for this adventure, and after your failure Trotsky rushed back to Petrograd to drive new martyrs to slaughter - for cheaply he gets our workers' and peasants' blood!....

Kronstadt lived in deep faith that the proletariat of Petrograd would come to its aid. But the workers there were terrorised, and Kronstadt effectively blockaded and isolated, so that in reality no assistance could be expected from anywhere.

The Kronstadt garrison consisted of less than 14,000 men, 10,000 of them being sailors. The garrison had to defend a widespread front, many forts and batteries scattered over the vast area of the Gulf. The repeated attacks of the Bolsheviks, whom the Central Government continuously supplied with fresh troops; the lack of provisions in the besieged city; the long sleepless nights spent on guard in the cold - all were sapping the vitality of Kronstadt. Yet the sailors heroically persevered, confident to the last that their great example of liberation would be followed throughout the country and thus bring them relief and aid.

In its 'Appeal to Comrades Workers and Peasants' the Provisional Revolutionary Committee says (*Izvestia* number 9, March 11);

> Comrades Workers, Kronstadt is fighting for you, for the hungry,

the cold, the naked....Kronstadt has raised the banner of rebellion and it is confident that tens of millions of workers and peasants will respond to its call. It cannot be that the daybreak which has begun in Kronstadt should not become bright sunshine for the whole of Russia. It cannot be that the Kronstadt explosion should fail to arouse the whole of Russia and first of all, Petrograd.

But no help was coming, and with every successive day Kronstadt was growing more exhausted. The Bolsheviks continued massing fresh troops against the beseiged fortress and weakening it by constant attacks. Moreover, every advantage was on the side of the Communists, including numbers, supplies, and position. Kronstadt had not been built to sustain an assault from the rear. The rumour spread by the Bolsheviks that the sailors meant to bombard Petrograd was false on the face of it. The famous fortress had been planned with the sole view of serving as a defence of Petrograd against foreign enemies approaching from the sea. Moreover, in case the city should fall into the hands of an external enemy, the coast batteries and forts of Krasnaia Gorka had been calculated for a fight **against** Kronstadt. Foreseeing such a possibility, the builders had purposely failed to strengthen the rear of Kronstadt.

Almost nightly the Bolsheviks continued their attacks. All through March 10 Communist artillery fired incessantly from the southern and northern coasts. On the night of 12 - 13 the Communists attacked from the south, again resorting to the white shrouds and sacrificing many hundreds of the *kursanti*. Kronstadt fought back desperately, in spite of many sleepless nights, lack of food and men. It fought most heroically against simultaneous assaults from the north, east and south, while the Kronstadt batteries were capable of defending the fortress only from its western side. The sailors lacked even an ice-cutter to make the approach of the Communist forces impossible.

On March 16 the Bolsheviks made a concentrated attack from three sides at once - from north, south and east. 'The plan of attack', later explained Dibenko, formerly Bolshevik naval Commissar and later dictator of defeated Kronstadt, 'was worked out in minutest detail according to the directions of Commander-in-Chief Tukhachevsky and the field staff of the Southern Corps....At dark we began the attack on the forts. The white shrouds and the courage of the *kursanti* made it possible for us to advance in columns'.

On the morning of March 17 a number of forts had been taken. Through the weakest spot of Kronstadt - the Petrograd Gates - the Bolsheviks broke into the city, and then there began most brutal slaughter. The Communists spared by the sailors now betrayed them, attacking from the rear. Commissar of the Baltic Fleet Kuzmin and Chairman of the Kronstadt Soviet Vassiliev, liberated by the Communists from jail, now participated in the hand to hand street fighting in fratricidal bloodshed. Till late in the night continued the desperate struggle of the Kronstadt sailors and soldiers against overwhelming odds. The city which for 15 days had not harmed a single Communist, now ran red with the blood of Kronstadt men, women and even children.

Dibenko, appointed Commissar of Kronstadt, was vested with absolute powers to 'clean the mutinous city'. An orgy of revenge followed, with the Cheka claiming numerous victims for its nightly wholesale *razstrel* (shooting).

On March 18 the Bolshevik Government and the Communist Party of Russia publicly commemorated the Paris Commune of 1871, drowned in the blood of the French workers by Gallifet and Thiers. At the same time they celebrated the 'victory' over Kronstadt.

For several weeks the Petrograd jails were filled with hundreds of Kronstadt prisoners. Every night small groups of them were taken out by order of the Cheka and disappeared - to be seen among the living no more. Among the last to be shot was Perepelkin, member of the Provisional Revolutionary Committee of Kronstadt.

The prisons and concentration camps in the frozen district of Archangel and the dungeons of far Turkestan are slowly doing to death the Kronstadt men who rose against Bolshevik bureaucracy and proclaimed in March, 1921, the slogan of the Revolution of October, 1917; 'All Power to the Soviets!'

Author's Afterword

Lessons and Significance of Kronstadt

The Kronstadt movement was spontaneous, unprepared, and peaceful. That it became an armed conflict, ending in a bloody tragedy, was entirely due to the Tartar despotism of the Communist dictatorship.

Though realising the general character of the Bolsheviks, Kronstadt, still had faith in the possibility of an amicable solution. It believed the Communist Government amenable to reason; it credited it with some sense of justice and liberty.

The Kronstadt experience proves once more that government, the State - whatever its name or form - is ever the mortal enemy of liberty and popular self-determination. The State has no soul, no principles. It has but one aim - to secure power and to hold it, at any cost. That is the political lesson of Kronstadt.

There is another, a strategic, lesson taught by every rebellion.

The success of an uprising is conditioned in its resoluteness, energy, and aggressiveness. The rebels have on their side the sentiment of the masses. That sentiment quickens with the rising tide of rebellion. It must not be allowed to subside, to pale by a return to the drabness of everyday life.

On the other hand, every uprising has against it the powerful machinery of the State. The Government is able to concentrate in its hands the sources of supply and the means of communication. No time must be given the Government to make use of its powers. Rebellion should be vigorous, striking unexpectedly and determinedly. It must not remain localised, for that means stagnation. It must broaden and develop. A rebellion that localises itself, plays the waiting policy, or puts itself on the defensive, is inevitably doomed to defeat.

In this regard, especially, Kronstadt repeated the fatal strategic errors of the Paris Communards. The latter did not follow the advice of those who favoured an immediate attack on Versailles while the Government of Thiers was disorganised. They did not carry the revolution into the country. Neither the Paris workers of 1871 nor the Kronstadt sailors aimed to abolish the Government. The Communards wanted merely certain Republican liberties, and when the Government attempted to disarm them, they drove the Ministers of Thiers from Paris, established their liberties and prepared to defend them - nothing more. Thus also Kronstadt demanded only free elections to the Soviets. Having arrested a few Commissars, the sailors prepared to defend themselves against attack. Kronstadt refused to act on the advice of the military experts immediately to take Oranienbaum. The latter was of utmost military value, besides having over 800,000 tonnes of wheat belonging to Kronstadt. A landing in Oranienbaum was feasible, the Bolsheviks having been taken by surprise and having had no time to bring up reinforcements. But the sailors did not want to take the offensive, and thus the psychologic moment was lost. A few days afterward, when the declarations and acts of the Bolshevik Government convinced Kronstadt that they were involved in a struggle for life, it was too late to make good the error.*

The same happened to the Paris Commune. When the logic of the fight forced upon them demonstrated the necessity of abolishing the Thiers regime not only in their own city but in the whole country, it was too late. In the Paris Commune as in the Kronstadt uprising the **tendency toward passive, defensive tactics proved fatal.**

Kronstadt fell. The Kronstadt movement for free Soviets was stifled in blood, while at the same time the Bolshevik Government was making compromises with European capitalists, signing the Riga peace, according to which a population of 12 millions was turned over to the mercies of Poland, and helping Turkish imperialism to suppress the republics of the Caucasus.

But the 'triumph' of the Bolsheviks over Kronstadt held within itself the defeat of Bolshevism. It exposed the true character of the Communist dictatorship. The Communists proved themselves willing to sacrifice Communism, to make almost any compromise with international capitalism, yet refused the just demands of their own people - demands that voiced the October slogans of the Bolsheviks themselves; Soviets elected by direct and secret ballot, according to the Constitution of the Russian Socialist Federal Soviet Republic; and freedom of speech and press for the revolutionary parties.

The 10th All-Russian Congress of the Communist Party was in session in Moscow at the time of the Kronstadt uprising. At that

* The failure of Krondstadt to take Oranienbaum gave the Government an opportunity to strengthen the fortress with its trusted regiments, eliminate the 'infected' parts of the garrison, and execute the leaders of the aerial squadron which was about to join the Kronstadt rebels. Later the Bolsheviks used the fortress as a vantage point of attack against Kronstadt.

Among those executed in Oranienbaum were; Kolossov, division chief of the Red Navy airmen and chairman of the Provisional Revolutionary Committee just organised in Oranienbaum; Balabanov, secretary of the Committee, and Committee members Romanov, Vladimirov, etc. (A. B.)

Congress the whole Bolshevik economic policy was changed as a result of the Kronstadt events and the similarly threatening attitude of the people in various other parts of Russia and Siberia. The Bolsheviks preferred to reverse their basic policies, to abolish the *razverstka* (forcible requisition), introduce freedom of trade, give concessions to capitalists and give up Communism itself - the Communism for which the October Revolution was fought, seas of blood shed, and Russia brought to ruin and despair - but not to permit freely chosen Soviets.

Can anyone still question what the true purpose of the Bolsheviks was? Did they pursue Communist Ideals or Government Power?

Kronstadt is of great historic significance. It sounded the death knell of Bolshevism with its Party dictatorship, mad centralisation, Cheka terrorism and bureaucratic castes. It struck into the very heart of Communist autocracy. At the same time it shocked the intelligent and honest minds of Europe and America into a critical examination of Bolshevik theories and practices. It exploded the Bolshevik myth of the Communist State being the 'Workers' and Peasants' Government'. It proved that the Communist Party dictatorship and the Russian Revolution are opposites, contradictory and mutually exclusive. It demonstrated that the Bolshevik regime is unmitigated tyranny and reaction, and that the Communist State is itself the most potent and dangerous counter-revolution.

Kronstadt fell. But it fell victorious in its idealism and moral purity, its generosity and higher humanity. Kronstadt was superb. It justly prided itself on not having shed the blood of its enemies, the Communists within its midst. It had no executions. The untutored, unpolished sailors, rough in manner and speech, were too noble to follow the Bolshevik example of vengeance; they would not shoot even the hated Commissars. Kronstadt personified the generous, all-forgiving spirit of the Slavic soul and the century-old emancipation movement of Russia.

Kronstadt was the **first** popular and entirely independent attempt at liberation from the yoke of State Socialism - an attempt made directly by the people, by the workers, soldiers and sailors themselves. It was the first step toward the Third Revolution which is inevitable and which, let us hope, may bring to long-suffering Russia lasting freedom and peace.

This book was brought out by Phoenix Press and is the beginning of what we intend to be a continuing programme of libertarian publishing. We do not pay wages to ourselves and in the unlikely circumstance that any profits are made they will be used solely to promote libertarian publishing. We raise money by borrowing returnable loans (rather than soliciting non-returnable donations) and those who support us in this way get a copy of the relevant book plus, provided we manage to sell enough copies, the offer of their money back. If you want to know more about Phoenix Press, write to us at:-

BM Bookserv
London WC1N 3XX